A Special Gift

To _____

From _____

Father of My Heart

Janette Oke

BETHANY HOUSE PUBLISHERS
MINNEAPOLIS, MINNESOTA 55438

Editorial development by Blue Water Ink,
Grand Rapids, Michigan.

Artwork by Roselyn B. Danner.

Published by Bethany House Publishers
A Ministry of Bethany Fellowship, Inc.
6820 Auto Club Road, Minneapolis, Minnesota 55438

Printed in the United States of America

Library of Congress Cataloging-in-Publication Data

Oke, Janette, 1935–
   [Seasons of the heart. Selections]
   Father of my heart / Janette Oke.
      p.   cm.
   Excerpts from the Seasons of the Heart series.
   1. Meditations. I. Title.
BV4832.2.0415   1990
242—dc20   90–45473
ISBN 1-55661-155-2   CIP

FOREWORD

Joshua Jones was a young boy with a "different" family. Instead of the usual Dad, Mom, and children, Josh was raised by an aunt, grandfather, great uncle, and, as added support, an elderly great grandfather.

Though Josh went through a time of feeling "cheated" that he had no memories of his mother and father, he soon realized that in being loved and cared for he was blessed.

Josh faced many problems as a teen-ager. Questions that teens through the years have asked, Josh also had to answer within himself. Is Scripture true? Was the world created by an omnipotent God? If He created us, does He still care? What occupation or ministry has He chosen for me? Who will be my life partner? How will I know the right one?

A faithful God was with Josh in all his difficult decisions and in the trying times that were beyond his control. Even when things were at their darkest and Josh, alone, could only pray and ask God to take total control of his topsy-turvy world, God was faithful.

For those of us who share the story of Josh, the beautiful reality is that God is *still* faithful. He does care and is still in control of our lives when we allow Him to be.

Janette Oke

CONTENTS

ONCE UPON
A SUMMER

THINKIN'

I could hardly wait to finish my chores. I needed to sneak off to the crik bank for some thinkin' time. I was worried that my whole world was about to change. I liked things jest the way they were, and if I was to keep 'em that way, it was going to take some figurin' out.

The crik was high, but the spot I called mine was a quiet place. Funny how it *feels* quiet, even though there isn't a still moment. One bird song followed another, and all sorts of bugs buzzed continually. Occasionally a frog would croak from the shallows or a fish would jump in the deeper waters. That kind of noise didn't bother me, though. I still found the spot restful, mostly 'cause there weren't any human voices biddin' ya to do this or git that.

Before I sat down on my log, I rolled up my overalls and let my feet slip into the cool crik water. I pushed my feet down deep, stretchin' my toes through the thin layer of coarse sand so I could wiggle them around in the mud beneath, and then I sat there trying to decide jest what angle to come at my problems from. [9–10]

A quiet place is a good place to find out
God's angle on any problem.

Think on these things.
PHILIPPIANS 4:8

SORROW

Grandpa backed the team out and we headed for home. When we were outside of town, he handed the reins to me.

"I'm kinda anxious to see what my pa be sayin'," he explained. He read the letter in silence, and I stole a glance at him now and then. It didn't seem to be pleasin' Grandpa much. Finally he folded it and tucked it away.

"Yer great-granny jest passed away, Boy."

He reached for the reins again in an absentminded way. If he'd really been thinkin', he would have let me keep drivin'—he most often did on the way back from town.

I was sorry to hear about Great-granny, but I couldn't claim to sorrow. I had never met her and had heard very little about her. Suddenly it hit me that it was different for Grandpa. That faraway old lady who had jest died was his ma. I felt a lump come up in my throat then—a kind of feelin' fer Grandpa—but I didn't know how to tell him how I felt.   [11–12]

When we can feel someone else's pain,
we can help to lessen it.

Comfort him, lest perhaps such a one should
be swallowed up with overmuch sorrow.
2 CORINTHIANS 2:7

REGRET

Grandpa was deep in thought. I could imagine right then that he was rememberin' Great-granny as he had seen her last. Many times he'd told me that when he was fifteen, he'd decided that he wanted to get away from the city. So he had packed up the few things that were rightly his, bid good-bye to his folks, and struck out for the West. Great-granny had cried as she watched him go, but she hadn't tried to stop him. Grandpa had been west for many years when he invited Uncle Charlie, his older and only brother to join him. Uncle Charlie was a bachelor, and he was glad to leave his job as a hardware-store clerk and travel west to join his brother.

Every year or so the two of them would sit and talk about payin' a visit back home, but they never got around to doin' it. Now Great-granny was gone, and Great-grandpa was left on his own—an old man. [12–13]

*We will never regret doing the things
we know we should do.*

The statutes of the LORD are right,
rejoicing the heart.
PSALM 19:8

MOTHERLESS

B oy," Grandpa said to me, "you and me have another thing in common now—the hurt of havin' no ma."

He started talkin' then. I had rarely heard my grandpa talk so much at one time.

"Funny how so many memories come stealin' back fresh as if they'd jest happened. Haven't thought on them fer years, but they're still there fer jest sech a time. Yer great-granny was one of the kindest, gentlest people I ever knew. Jest the touch of her hand brushed the fever from ya. And when she gathered ya into her arms in her old rockin' chair after she had washed ya all up fer bed, and held ya close against her, and rocked back and forth hummin' an old hymn and kissin' yer hair—"

Grandpa stopped and swallowed, and a tear slid down his cheek.

"Shucks," he said, "I knew that I was too old fer that, but as long as the neighbor kids didn't catch me at it. Funny how loved I felt. Then one day I knew that I was jest too big to be hugged and rocked anymore—but I missed it, and I think Mama did, too."   [13–14]

No one ever outgrows the need for a mother's love.

Isaac was comforted after his mother's death.
GENESIS 24:67

MEMORIES

Grandpa had forgotten all about the team that he was supposed to be drivin', and the horses were takin' every advantage given them. No horse could have gone any slower and still have been puttin' one foot in front of the other. Every now and then Old Bell would reach down and steal a mouthful of grass without really stoppin' to graze. Nellie didn't particularly seem to mind goin' slowly either.

I watched the horses and glanced back at Grandpa, wondering jest how long he was going to put up with the situation. I think he had even forgotten *me*. I could tell that his mind was still mullin' over old memories. Many of them had been happy ones, but they brought sadness now that they were never to be again.

Suddenly Grandpa roused himself and turned to me.

"Memories are beautiful things, Boy. When the person ya love is gone, when the happy time is over, ya still have yer memories. Thank God fer this special gift of His. Ain't no price one would settle on fer the worth of memories."   [14–15]

If we savor the good times in youth,
we can enjoy them again in old age.

They shall abundantly utter the memory
of thy great goodness.
PSALM 145:7

UGLY FEELINGS

Grandpa could go on and on about things he recalled from his childhood: his mother's face, her smile, her smell, her touch. Me, all I had was a great big blank spot—only a name—Agatha.

Sometimes I laid awake at night tryin' to put a face to that name, but I never could. When I was younger I'd watch the faces of ladies and when I found one I liked I'd pretend that was the way my mother's face had looked.

A sick feelin' began to knot up my stomach, and I felt a little angry with God. Why did He think it fair to take my parents when I was only a baby and not even leave me with memories like other folks had? Wasn't it bad enough to be a kid without a mom to hug him or a pa to go fishin' with him?

I didn't dare look at Grandpa. I was afraid he'd look right through me and see the ugly feelings inside.   [15–16]

> *Ugly feelings that we try to hide inside us
> eventually surface as ugly behavior.*

He that covereth his sins shall not prosper.
PROVERBS 28:13

PRAYER

I backed slowly out of the door and tip-toed to my room. I couldn't believe what I had heard. Grandpa and Uncle Charlie were trying to get Auntie Lou married. They wanted Great-grandpa to come live with us, and they didn't want Lou to have to take care of all of us men. There had to be a way I could stop this.

An idea flashed through my mind—prayer. I'd already said my evenin' prayers, but this one was extra. "Dear God," I prayed. "You know what they're plannin' fer Auntie Lou, but I want to keep her. You didn't let me keep my ma—or my pa. Now you gotta help me to find a way to keep Aunt Lou. And about Great-grandpa—maybe you could find him a new wife, even if he is old, so that he won't need to come here. Or maybe he could die on the train comin' out or somethin'. Anyway, please do what you can, God. You sorta owe me a favor after all you've taken from me. Amen."

Satisfied that I had done what I could, I crawled into bed. I wasn't sure God would pay too much attention to my prayer, but I'd tried. Tomorrow I'd work on a plan of my own in case God decided not to do anything for me. [24–25]

> *We can expect big trouble when*
> *we try to answer our own prayers.*

For a pretence make . . . prayer.
MATTHEW 23:14

17

CONSCIENCE

Lou didn't seem upset to hear that Great-grandpa was plannin' to come. In fact, she looked pleased and excited about it. Maybe she wouldn't leave us. It wasn't until I had been threatened with losing Auntie Lou that I realized just how important she was to me.

Jest as I started to feel better, I remembered parts of my prayer. If God took me seriously, I had the feelin' He didn't care much for some of what I'd been askin' for. My conscience started a-prickin' at me. I had some correctin' to do.

"Dear God, I wanta thank ya for spendin' yer time and energy working on my prayer. Please, can ya jest forget that part 'bout havin' him die on the train? It's okay if he comes—I guess. And don't bother 'bout a new wife. He'd jest bring her, too, and we sure don't need that. Thank ya. Amen."

I felt a little better then. I wasn't sure if it was God I feared or my family—should they ever find out that I had brought down fire from heaven on a man they loved and wanted. Anyway, God and I had it sorted out now, so there wasn't much need to worry over it any longer. [36–37]

Confession is the only way
to correct a corrupt conscience.

Now therefore make confession
unto the LORD God.
EZRA 10:11

FAMILY

Y ou'll never know how many times on my train ride out here that I thanked the Lord for my family," Great-grandpa said. "Must be the most awful thing in the world not to have *anybody*. I felt at first that I had no one—when Mama died—but all I needed to do was to make connections again. Some people aren't that fortunate. When their partner is gone, they are alone—really alone.

"Here I am with my family—two sons, a granddaughter, and a great-grandson. My family. I am a man mightily blessed."

I had some thanks that needed sayin', too—thanks that God hadn't taken me seriously when I wanted to get rid of this wonderful old man. It almost made me break into a sweat to think of what I had been eager to deny myself.

Gramps talked about his "family." Sure we were a family. You didn't have to be a ma and a pa and four kids to be a family. All you needed was people livin' together and lovin' and helpin' one another. That's what made a family—blood-ties and love-bonds. I straightened up taller in my chair. I was right proud to be a member of this family. [72]

The blessing of an earthly family gives us only a hazy picture of the blessing in God's heavenly family.

Children's children are the crown of old men;
and the glory of children are their fathers.
PROVERBS 17:6

CHANGE

When the sun had been up long enough to dry the grain bundles, the lead team moved out. Men rode along and forked on the bundles as the team moved slowly down the field, stoppin' and startin' at the command of their owner.

As soon as they had enough to test they returned to the threshin' machine. That's when things really came to life. The steam engine roared and trembled. The gears clashed and banged on the threshin' machine as it picked up its pace. It seemed to rock and stomp like an angry dragon.

At the nod of the machine operator, the team moved in close to the machine, and the bundle pitchers went into motion, too, tossin' the bundles onto the belts that carried them up and fed them into the belly of the big machine.

That was where the miracle took place. Instead of comin' out chopped and mutilated, streams of clean grain began pouring into the box of the wagon. A small cloud puffed from the spout that blew away the straw; the cloud grew and became shimmering gold and silver flashes as the sun hit the flying particles.

I always stood in awe. It never ceased to amaze me, this sudden and well-ordered change. [93–94]

The changes in nature remind us of the glorious transformation that's coming for all believers.

We shall all be changed.
1 CORINTHIANS 15:51

HELPFULNESS

Gramps and I talked as we waited for a fish to strike. "You know, Joshua," said Gramps, "I've been thinking that I've hit the best years of a man's life. Take you now. Sure you've got your delights—your fishing, your lack of adult worries; but you've got your schooling, and you work hard, too."

I was glad Gramps had noticed.

"Your Grandpa and Uncle Charlie have men's work and worries. Takes most of their time and energy to just keep up with things. But *me*," he sighed and leaned back against the warm tree trunk. "Me—I don't have to go to school or even chore if I don't feel like it. No sirree, Joshua. I've got it made."

I'd never considered that there were advantages to being old. It sounded pretty good all right, but not quite accurate for Gramps. I'd seen him feed the chickens, pump water, and tote wood. I'd also seen him with his shirt sleeves rolled up, peeling vegetables, drying dishes, or sweeping the floor.

Maybe he didn't *have* to do those things; but knowin' Gramps, I had the feelin' that as long as he could still totter, he'd be doin' what he could to lighten someone's load. He was a great old guy, my Gramps. [95–96]

When our load is light,
it's time to carry someone else's.

He is our help.
PSALM 33:20

SHARING MEMORIES

Gramps started tellin' me all about Great-grandma—rememberin' little things that probably seemed insignificant when they happened. It was easy for me to feel his loss—I'd lost family, too.

We fished in silence for a while and then decided it was time for lunch. We had jest lifted cold chicken drumsticks from the pail when I sensed a commotion in the water; Gramps had a fish. He jumped up, dropped his chicken, and went whoopin' and yellin' down the bank. I joined him. We were shoutin' and dancin' and callin' to one another. Gramps landed one of the nicest fish I'd ever seen taken from the crik.

We went home happy.

"Glad we were able to fit this day in, Joshua," Gramps said.

"Me too."

"You're good company. Hope you didn't mind an old man sharing some memories."

I looked at him. " 'Course not." Shucks! Why should I mind sharin' Gramps's memories? Especially since I didn't have any of my own. [96–97]

We never know which things we do will stay forever in our minds, so it's best to choose each action carefully.

O my God, my soul is cast down within me: therefore will I remember thee.
PSALM 42:6

CONTROL

Thursday came. We were all able to let out the breath that we'd been holdin'. There's always the threat of bad weather movin' in on a threshin' operation. It delays the plans and makes big men sweat with worry over something they have no power to do a thing about. Used to be I'd pray for days on end before threshin', pleadin' with the Lord to favor us with fittin' weather. Last year a bad storm moved in on us in spite of my prayers, so this year I decided that I would jest leave the Lord on His own. [98]

We can influence God through prayer,
but we can't control Him.

Hath not the potter power over the clay?
ROMANS 9:21

THE GIFT

Got something to show you, Joshua," Gramps said. "Come with me."

Gramps led the way to the small shed that stood in the yard. I wasn't much interested in seein' anything in there, but I followed. Maybe Gramps had found a mouse nest or something.

As Gramps opened the door a funny bit of black and white fur came flyin' at my feet. I jumped like lightnin' had jest warmed my boots. Gramps was chucklin' and scoopin' up the wiggly thing, tryin' to get it under control.

I took a better look then, and my breath caught in my throat. It was a pup. I reached out for it, my head full of questions.

Gramps smiled real wide. "He's yours, Joshua."

My mind couldn't comprehend it, but my arms were already claimin' possession. I pushed my face against the ball of fur and had my face licked as a thank you for noticin' him. I laughed and got licked again. He wasn't still for a moment, and I could see that he was going to be an awful lot of fun.

"My dog! My very own dog!" I kept sayin' over and over to myself, hardly able to believe my good fortune.   [115–116]

*An undeserved and unexpected gift is
the most pleasant to give and to receive.*

Every good gift and every perfect gift
is from above.
JAMES 1:17

GOD KNOWS BEST

After supper I took some meat scraps and a saucer of milk to Patches. I begged an old jacket off Uncle Charlie and fixed Patches a comfortable bed in a box low enough for him to come and go as he wanted.

I was called for bed way too soon. I promised Patches that I'd be down first thing in the mornin'. I went to bed with my mind full of plans for my dog—the doghouse I'd build, the collar I'd make him, the tricks I'd teach him. There was a whole new world waitin' for me now—and all because of Gramps.

I hadn't been talkin' much to God lately, and I was a little hesitant now about prayin' after ignorin' Him for so long. But I finally crawled out of bed and got down on my knees.

"Dear God, I wanna say thank you for a few things. I know sometimes I don't think you're doin' much special-like for me, but I do wanna thank you for bringin' Gramps here—even iffen I didn't want him at first. I really love him now, God. And thank you for Patches, too. Help me to make him a good dog so that he won't be *too* much of a nuisance. Amen." [117–118]

We do not always know the reasons for what God does and doesn't do, but in the end we'll see that He was always right.

At the name of Jesus every knee should bow.
PHILIPPIANS 2:10

CARING

Auntie Lou bit her lip to fight back tears. Finally she was able to talk. "A bad thing happened today, Josh. Your puppy was killed."

It couldn't be true, it jest couldn't. But a look at Gramps's white face told me that I had to believe it.

I jumped up from the table, spillin' my milk, and ran for the door. I ran all the way to the crik. I wished that I could jest throw myself right into the cold water and let it wash all the feelin' from me. Boys weren't supposed to cry—but I cried. I cried until my eyes ran dry, and then I jest laid there and groaned.

It was gettin' dark when I finally lifted myself from the bank. I was shiverin'. I knelt down by the stream and sloshed cold water over my face again and again. It nearly froze me but it sharpened things back into focus, too. I hadn't done one bit of my chores. I started home at a trot.

When I got to the house, I found that Gramps had done all of my chores. Auntie Lou had milked Bossie and helped to split the wood. It made me feel shame—but a great deal of love and gratitude, too. [120–121]

> *People who care find ways to share*
> *other people's sorrow.*

And went to him . . . and took care of him.
LUKE 10:34

BITTERNESS

Gramps sat quietly on my bed for a while and then he reached out an old hand and touched my arm.

"I know how you hurt, Joshua. It's not easy to lose someone you love."

I gulped. If he wasn't careful I'd be cryin' again.

"Patches was a busy little dog—and a smart one. But I guess he just figured that he knew a little more than he really did. The range cattle were pasturing just across the fence from the garden, and Patches decided that he'd be a cattle dog. Anyway, Lou and I heard the ruckus, but by the time we got there he'd been kicked. We tried to save him but—"

Tears came again and I swallowed them away.

Gramps patted me gently, got up, and moved toward the door. I was glad he hadn't expected me to talk.

I laid there thinkin' about my little dog, and then a lot of other thoughts started comin' to me. I used them like a blanket, wrappin' myself up in them and findin' a queer kind of satisfaction in the thought that I had suffered more than anyone else in the world. Bitterness filled me until I could hold no more. [122]

> *Wrapping ourselves in bitterness is like using*
> *a blanket of poison ivy;*
> *it's warm at first but painful in the end.*

Let all bitterness . . . be put away from you.
EPHESIANS 4:31

SELF-PITY

My door opened and Auntie Lou slipped in. "I'm sorry, Josh. There was jest no way we could have stopped it."

"God could've. I even prayed last night, and I thanked Him for Gramps and I thanked Him for Patches, and then without even waitin' He lets my dog die. He could have stopped it! He doesn't care. He jest hurts and hurts, and iffen He thinks I'm gonna love Him—I'm not—I won't. He doesn't even leave me memories," I almost shouted. "He takes everything."

Auntie Lou took my hand and stroked it gently.

"God took my ma and pa, too, before I could have any memories. Everybody's got memories but me."

"Josh, my mama died before I was old enough to remember her, but I have lots of memories, and they're jest as filled with love. I remember Pa bringing home a tiny baby all wrapped in blankets. With tears in his eyes he gave him to me and said he was mine to care for. I remember dressin' him and feedin' him and playin' with him—and lovin' him. I have lots of memories, Josh—lots of *good* memories."

Auntie Lou was right. I had some memories, too. I'd jest been lookin' in the wrong place for them.   [122–124]

Each of us must choose what to remember—
the good or the bad times of life.

I am full of heaviness: and I looked for some
to take pity, but there was none.
PSALM 69:20

HURT

I was fightin' an inward battle now. I was still angry and wantin' to strike back.

"God still didn't need to take my dog."

"Josh, God *didn't* take your dog. It was jest—jest one of those things that happens, that's all."

"But He coulda *stopped* it."

"Yes, He could have. He could protect us from everything that would hurt us. I could do that with my petunias, Josh. I could build a box around them and keep them from the wind and the rain, the crawlers and the bees. But they'd never bear flowers iffen I did," said Auntie Lou. "Josh, I don't understand all about God, but as sure as I live and breathe I know God loves us completely and always keeps our good in mind. I don't know how losin' your pup is for your good, Josh, but I *am* sure that it *can* be. It's all up to you, Josh. Whenever something comes into our life that hurts us, we do the decidin'—do I let this work for my good, as God intended, or do I let bitterness grow like a canker sore in my soul? We can't change what's happened, Josh. But don't give the hurt a chance to grow even bigger and destroy you." [124–125]

How we respond to hurt determines whether our spirits will grow and bloom or wither and die.

Having received the word in much affliction,
with joy of the Holy Ghost.
1 THESSALONIANS 1:6

CONFUSION

I laid there thinkin' of all that Auntie Lou had said. I decided that one day soon, maybe down by the crik, I'd work on some memories and see jest what I could come up with. Even as I laid there I saw a blue-eyed, laughin' face bendin' over me, cooin' love words—my Auntie Lou. I pushed it aside. I didn't want to get love feelin's all mixed in with my bitter ones. The one might somehow destroy the other.

Auntie Lou loved me, of that I had no question. So did Gramps, and even, I was willin' to admit, Grandpa and Uncle Charlie. But God? Somehow that jest didn't add up.

If He did love me He sure chose some strange ways of showin' it. I knew that Auntie Lou wouldn't want me to hate God. I was even a little afraid of the consequences myself. No, I decided, I wouldn't hate Him—but I couldn't love Him either. I'd jest feel nothin'—nothin' at all. I wouldn't even think about Him. I'd jest ignore Him completely. That would give Him something to think about. Maybe He'd even feel sorry.   [125]

> *If we nurture bitterness it will destroy love;*
> *if we nurture love, it will destroy bitterness.*

We are perplexed, but not in despair.
2 CORINTHIANS 4:8

IMPORTANCE

Nothin' of much importance happened at church, but I knew I had to go; it was one of Grandpa's unwritten laws. But there wasn't much he could do to make me listen. I did pull my attention back for a few minutes when Mr. T. Smith, the chairman of the church board, stepped to the front. He cleared his throat and tried to look like he didn't consider that position as elevated *too* much above the rest.

"You all know thet our good pastor and his wife have expressed a desire to retire," he said. "We will miss them deeply, but we know thet they have earned the right to some rest. Although we will miss the Whites, we are happy to announce that yer church board has been successful in findin' a replacement. The Reverend Nathaniel Crawford will come to take Reverend White's place. We trust that you will all make him welcome and give him yer support."

Nathaniel Crawford, I thought. What a name! I dismissed the new preacher as not worth thinkin' on and went back to my day-dreamin'. It all had very little to do with me.   [146–147]

What seems unimportant one day
may be of utmost significance the next.

He is not here, but is risen: remember how he
spake unto you when he was yet in Galilee.
LUKE 24:6

CONVICTION

Reverend White started his message after the announcement of his retirement. I listened for jest a minute or two to find out what I'd be missin'. It was on repentin' again. I'd heard that before. This time he was usin' poor ol' Paul as his example of a wicked man turned good. Ol' Paul probably never had anything bothersome happen to him. Why shouldn't he be good? I let my mind wander.

The talk during Sunday dinner was about the new preacher. Folks were wonderin' where he was from, what he'd be like, and what he had for family. The only thing I wondered was if he'd still preach on "gettin' ready" and repentance and all. I didn't care much for those kinds of sermons. Something about them made me feel a queer twistin' deep on the inside of me.

I shrugged my shoulders. I really wasn't plannin' on listenin' much anyway, so I guessed it really didn't matter what he preached about. [147–148]

Putting God out of our minds
doesn't eliminate Him from our lives.

Whither shall I go from thy spirit? or whither
shall I flee from thy presence?
PSALM 139:7

Lou hadn't really fussed about the meal. It was the usual simple yet tasty fare that we normally enjoyed. The table was laid with the everyday dishes. It was clear to me that Auntie Lou wasn't out to impress the new preacher.

She acted the perfect hostess, though, quiet and polite, lookin' after those at her table, but no more. The parson seemed to enjoy the cookin'—especially the hot biscuits. He ate them until he seemed embarrassed and then ate another one anyway.

Like Auntie Lou, I didn't have too much to say during the meal. I was busy lookin' over this new preacher, tryin' to figure him out. I jest couldn't put my finger on any good reason why a young, manly fella like him would want to be a parson. There were so many other things that he could have chosen—like bein' a cowboy or a sheriff or a wrestler. But here he was, a preacher. I jest couldn't figure it out. I finally concluded that he must be a fair amount crazy—or at least a little slow. As I listened to the conversation, that theory didn't add up either. He seemed bright enough, and pleasant, too. It was all a puzzle to me. I felt real curiosity about the man. He was certainly a strange one. [154–155]

When we follow God,
people may question our direction.

They will not believe me . . . for they will
say, The LORD hath not appeared unto thee.
EXODUS 4:1

AMAZIN' GRACE

The new pastor took his place, and the attention shifted to him—especially that of the girls. He looked even taller and younger up there behind the pulpit. *Preacher has no business lookin' like that. He's supposed to be sorta world-worn and old lookin'.*

I was curious as to what this new preacher had to say. I didn't plan on really listenin'—jest sorta checkin' up on him.

When I summed it all up, I felt rather tricked. Really it was the same thing I'd been hearin' all my life—only put to us in a different way. "God's Glorious Provision" he called it. But one thing sorta had me puzzled. This preacher looked like what he was talkin' about filled him with such happiness that he was about to bust. It seemed that he was pleased to pieces that God had gone out of His way for man. "Mercy," he called it—mercy and grace—mercy bein' the withholdin' of what you *really* deserved, like a woodshed trip if you'd been bad; and grace—the gettin' of what you really didn't deserve, like the extra dish of ice cream when there were six servin's and five people.

At the end of the sermon we sang "Amazin' Grace," and a look at the preacher's face told everyone that he truly thought it was amazin'. [159–160]

*The old story of God's grace should be
new and fresh to us every day.*

And the grace of our Lord
was exceeding abundant.
1 TIMOTHY 1:14

35

SIN

As I was headin' by the parsonage, the preacher pulled up on his horse. He grinned from ear to ear when he saw me.

"Hi there, Josh. Right glad that I didn't miss you. Just let me put Big Jim away and we'll rustle up some milk and cookies. Do you mind if I grab my wash off the line on my way by?"

"Not at all. I'd help you iffen I didn't need to hang on to Pixie." Pixie was the new puppy Gramps gave me after Patches was killed.

The preacher asked for a report on Pixie's training as he gathered the clothes, and I told him about all her tricks.

He opened the door and let me into the house, then he laid his laundry carefully on the table and went about gettin' the milk and cookies. Pastor Nat took a drink of milk and then started matchin' socks. I noticed that most of the pairs had been mended—some of them many times. He came to a pair with a small hole in one toe and laid them aside.

"Guess I'd better take care of that one before I wear it again," he laughed. "Holes in socks are sorta like sin, Josh. If you don't tend to them when they're small, they grow with amazing speed." [163–165]

Confessing sin does more than just "patch up"
our lives; it gives us a brand new start.

I will confess my transgressions unto the LORD.
PSALM 32:5

VISION

P a died when I was twelve, so my ma had to take in wash to get by," Pastor Nat said. "Pa's cousin lived nearby—big man, big family, but not much energy. His place was rundown and dirty. Mama vowed that no matter how poor we were, our place would never look like that. So we both worked hard.

"It was my dream to be a preacher. Before my pa died he called both Mama and me in. 'Son,' he said, 'I know it looks a little dark right now, but if God truly wants you in His work, don't give up—there'll come a way.'

"Every time Mama could lay aside a few extra dollars from her washing, she would order another book for me to read—'to keep the vision fresh,' she would say.

"She was a great little woman, my mama. She used to worry that I had to become a man at twelve years of age, but I believe it was all in God's plan. I learned to make tough decisions quickly, and I learned the importance of following through on responsibilities." [165–166]

When our vision comes from God,
there is no doubt that we can accomplish it.

A vision appeared to Paul in the night; . . .
saying, Come over into Macedonia . . .
immediately we endeavored to go . . .
assuredly gathering that the Lord had called us.
ACTS 16:9–10

RUMORS

My wife's brother dropped by t'other day," I overheard Mr. Brown say to Grandpa. "He knows the Crawford family fairly well. He don't recall a Nathaniel, but he says there's so many kids that he never could git 'em straight. They's not too highly thought of. Shiftless, lazy, dirty—not much account. He couldn't believe one of 'em decided to be a preacher."

"Maybe he has the wrong family," said Grandpa.

"Only one there. Had been another but he and his wife are both buried there. Henry suggested that maybe this Nathaniel was a smart rascal that figured as how the ministry was an easy way to make a livin' without workin'."

"Don't know much about the ministry then!" Grandpa said. He was silent a minute before he continued. "Well, Lukus, I shore do hate to pass judgment on a man without givin' him a chance. There could be some mix-up here. And even if he is one and the same, we ain't leavin' any room fer the work of the Lord at all. He's restored a lot of no-good folks. We both know that." [167–168]

If we accept a rumor as fact, we encourage rumor spreaders, making it more likely that we too will become a victim of an untrue rumor.

But let none of you suffer as . . .
a busybody in other men's matters.
1 PETER 4:15

SEEDS OF DOUBT

From my place in the hay I was hard put not to jump up and let Grandpa know the truth: the parson was not from the same shiftless family; he had worked hard and shouldered responsibility to get where he was. But to do so would be to admit eavesdroppin' on an adult conversation right there in front of Deacon Brown. I figured there would be plenty of opportunity later to casually mention to Grandpa my unplanned visit with the parson. I held my breath as well as my tongue.

Mrs. Brown yoo-hooed from down the street, and Mr. Brown excused himself. As he turned to go, Grandpa said softly, "And Lukus, I see no need for this to pass on any further than jest us two—at least fer the present."

I could see that what Mr. Brown said truly bothered Grandpa. Sure he was willin' to give a man a fair chance, but even so, he was human, too, and some seeds of doubt had been sown.

I supposed that I was the only one around, beside the preacher himself, who knew the real truth, but it didn't seem too wise an idea for me to share my knowledge at the moment. I felt all mixed up—wantin' to defend the preacher and yet not knowin' quite how.   [167–169]

Sowing seeds of doubt brings a harvest of confusion,
misunderstanding, and hurt.

And if I have taken any thing from any man
by false accusation, I restore him fourfold.
LUKE 19:8

ASKING

This fella's jest a kid," Grandpa said. "An' he has nothin'—nothin'. Did ya see his suit? All pressed an' clean, sure, but so thin ya could walk through it—the best he's got, too."

"Ya don't judge a man by his clothes—even I know thet," answered Uncle Charlie.

"Thet ain't the point! Point is, he can't *afford* a better suit. And iffen ya start with nothin', you sure ain't gonna add much to it on a preacher's salary. The man doesn't even have him a rig to drive—jest a saddle-horse. You wanna see Lou dressed in worn-out clothes a hangin' on a-straddle a horse?"

"Now hold on," said Uncle Charlie. "You know how I feel 'bout Lou. You know what I'd like to see her have. I jest don't see how you can stop this thing that's brewin', that's all."

"I'll have a talk with her."

"A talk? Jest like that, a talk, and the girl will ferget she ever saw the fella?"

"No," Grandpa answered, "it won't be that simple; but Lou's a good girl. She'll respect my wishes. Iffen I ask her not to return the compliment of his favor, she'll abide by it."

"Shore she will. It may break her heart, but she will." [175]

> *When we get what we ask for*
> *we may lose what we love.*

We have added unto all our sins this evil,
to ask us a king.
1 SAMUEL 12:19

41

SILENCE

I had heard all Grandpa's arguments to Uncle Charlie. Not once had he mentioned the information passed on to him by Deacon Brown. I knew that Grandpa truly did want to be fair to the parson, but I also knew that it was nigh impossible for him to completely forget what he had heard. He loved Lou and he didn't want to take any chances.

I wanted to keep Lou at home, so I hoped Grandpa's talk would work. At the same time, I felt afraid. Somehow it looked like Auntie Lou would be hurt. I didn't want that. More than anything in the world I wanted her happy.

I could call Grandpa to my room and relate to him my entire conversation with the preacher, but then maybe he wouldn't bother havin' that talk with Auntie Lou. I felt all torn up inside. It didn't seem fair to the preacher for me to remain silent, and yet maybe my silence would help me keep Auntie Lou. I promised myself that after everything was settled I'd tell Grandpa what I knew about the preacher. Surely it wouldn't hurt him if I jest kept quiet for a time.　　　　　[176–177]

*When someone's good reputation needs defending,
it is not the time for silence.*

A time to keep silence, and a time to speak.
ECCLESIASTES 3:7

OPPORTUNITY

I really must be going," said the preacher. "I need a bath and some fresh clothes." He rose from the table and thanked Auntie Lou for the breakfast. "And I'm thankful, Mr. Jones, truly thankful that you didn't lose your home in the fire."

"And I'll never be able to thank *you* enough for the plan ya came up with and the way you worked to carry it out," Grandpa said. "Everywhere I looked, there you was, diggin' and trampin' and pitchin' water and fightin' with a wet sack. Any man that can think and fight like that ain't goin' to be stopped by the hard things in life. Yer gonna make a great preacher—and yer more than welcome in my home anytime."

The preacher extended his hand, his face lightin' up. He hesitated a moment and then hurried on, seemin' to sense that he mustn't miss this chance of a lifetime.

"This may seem like taking advantage of the situation, Mr. Jones, but I would like to request your permission to call on your daughter—not as a minister, sir," he added with a smile.

Grandpa smiled, too, and extended his hand. "And I'd be right proud to have you do that." [190–192]

Patience keeps us from running ahead of God.
Alertness keeps us from missing His opportunities.

As we have therefore opportunity,
let us do good unto all men.
GALATIANS 6:10

ANTICIPATING LOSS

Friday night the preacher came for supper. It was almost more than I could do to watch him watchin' Auntie Lou with that self-satisfied look in his eyes. *It's really true*, I thought. *God's gonna take away Auntie Lou, too.*

I excused myself from the table, sayin' that I didn't feel too well, and went up to my room. I laid on my bed for a long time tryin' to sort it all out. Auntie Lou came up with a worried look on her face and felt my forehead.

"You're not gonna be sick, are ya, Josh?" she asked.

"Naw," I said, "I'll be fine come mornin'."

She still looked unconvinced and leaned over me, fixin' my pillow and brushin' back my hair. For a moment I felt a sense of victory that I still had the power to pull her away from the preacher; then the anger filled me again.

"I love ya, Josh," she whispered, and then she was gone.

I cried then; I couldn't help it. I drew Pixie close and cried into her fur. At least I still had Pixie. If God would jest leave her alone—at least I'd have her to love.   [196]

The loss that we dread sometimes
brings us more than we had before.

Thomas saith unto him, Lord, we know not
whither thou goest; and how can we know
the way?
JOHN 14:5

THE ALTAR

I joined Avery and Willie in a corner of the churchyard where they were messin' around in the snow.

"Bet I could take off ol' Mr. T.'s hat," boasted Willie.

"Thought you been to the altar and prayed for God to forgive and help you," countered Avery. "Yer s'posed to be *good* now."

"Said *bet* I could, not thet I was gonna try."

"Does it really work?" asked Jack Berry. "Does goin' to the altar make ya feel different?"

"It ain't goin' to the altar," said Willie. "It's the prayin' thet makes the difference, and a fella can pray any place." I had the feelin' Willie was repeatin' what the preacher had said.

"But does it *work*?"

"Yeah," said Willie, and his eyes lit up. "Yeah, it really did. I used to feel mean and mixed up inside, and now thet I told God I was sorry and thet I wanted to quit bein' thet way, I feel," he shrugged, "kinda clean and not fightin'-mad anymore."

"Ya mean—kinda—*peace*."

"Yeah, I guess so," Willie answered.

We all stood around Willie. I suppose every one of us wished that we could feel the things he described. [198]

> *We all want peace, but few of us are willing*
> *to give up our pride and self-ambition to get it.*

> We have an altar, whereof they have no right
> to eat which serve the tabernacle.
> HEBREWS 13:10

45

RISK

The preacher was talking to Mrs. Adams when suddenly his head jerked up. Without excusin' himself he ran toward a team of horses hitched at the rail fence. I looked to see what was makin' him run so. There was Pixie, and she was runnin' under the spookiest horses around. They near went wild.

The preacher placed a hand on the nearest horse and spoke soothing words. Then, without waitin' for them to quiet down, he went right underneath. I was too scared to even holler. The horses pitched and plunged and then out from under them rolled the preacher, and he held Pixie in his arms. He tried not to limp when he walked toward me. He checked Pixie to make sure she had no broken bones, then handed her to me. I cuddled her close. "Ya coulda been killed," I said, finally finding my voice. "Are you OK?"

"Sure—I'm fine—just bumped a little. Don't bother mentioning it, all right?"

I nodded. "I didn't know that ya liked dogs so much that you'd risk yer life for one."

"I like dogs real well, Josh. But it wasn't for Pixie that I got her out. It was for *you.*"   [199–200]

Love takes risks.

[Love] beareth all things, believeth all things,
hopeth all things, endureth all things.
1 CORINTHIANS 13:7

LOVED

I know how you love Pixie, Josh, and I know how a fella can feel *cheated* when he loses what he loves. You've already lost your ma and pa, and then you lost your first dog. Lou told me all about it. Pretty soon you'll be called on to share the most important person in your life, Josh. You might feel like you're losing her, too—but you won't be. Lou will always love you—always. She's worried about you, Josh. She's afraid you might not understand, that you'll be hurt and grow bitter. Lou is afraid you blamed God for your first dog being killed. She's afraid she couldn't make you understand that God loves you. Things happen in life that seem wrong and are painful, but it isn't because God *likes* to see us suffer. He wants to see us *grow*. He wants us to love Him, to trust Him."

"Can we go somewhere private a minute?" I asked.

"Sure," he said. He placed an arm around my shoulder, and we went through the side door into his study.

I poured out how I'd doubted God, blamed God, even tried to ignore Him. Then we prayed together. Willie Corbin was right. It did work! I felt clean and forgiven—and even better yet, *loved*.   [200–201]

Accepting God's love enables us to love others.

Hereby perceive we the love of God, because
he laid down his life for us: and we ought to
lay down our lives for the brethren.
1 JOHN 3:16

THE WINDS
OF AUTUMN

BAD LUCK

T his trip isn't what we expected, is it?" Willie asked.

I looked at him in silence. I wasn't sure just how much I was willing to admit—even to myself. Maybe camping wasn't all it was cracked up to be.

"Can't say Avery's had the best time in the world either," Willie continued. "I mean, who'd care to be chased by a bull or get dunked in a cold crik? But I've been thinkin' that maybe God arranged this trip. Did you know that Avery is painin' inside? He never says much—but yesterday when you were gone to the spring we got to talkin' an' Avery said what he was feelin'. His mom's been awful sick, an' he already lost a brother. He's scared, Josh. He's got this silly notion that God is out to hurt him. He's sure his mom is gonna die—an' he thinks it's his fault. We gotta help him, Josh. Show him that God really does love *him*."

I nodded. If we hadn't had all of our "bad luck," Willie wouldn't have had the chance to talk and pray with Avery like he did. We still wouldn't have known that Avery needed special friendship at this time. [60–61]

What we consider "bad luck"
may be part of God's sovereign plan.

The LORD maketh poor, and maketh rich:
he bringeth low, and lifteth up.
1 SAMUEL 2:7

YOUTH

Wafting out of the kitchen window of the Turley house was the most wonderful smell. Mrs. Turley was baking apple pie. Avery stepped up to the door and rapped gently. "Come in. Come in," said Mrs. Turley to her daughter, and we followed her into the kitchen.

"What can we do for you, boys?" she asked.

"We'd like a drink, please," responded Avery.

"Mary, get the boys some cold milk," said Mrs. Turley, and she went back to rolling out piecrust. "Never did care for milk all on its own," Mrs. Turley went on. "Mary, slice them some fresh bread and get out some of that strawberry jam. So you been campin'. Where'd ya go?"

"Up to the crik mouth, ma'am. We'd never been there," answered Willie.

"Neither have I," said Mrs. Turley, "an' I don't plan to waste no time in goin' way up there either." Then she smiled. "But I guess young boys with energy to spare don't quite look at things the way a tired ol' woman does." [63–64]

What seems important in youth
may seem silly later.

In length of days [is] understanding.
JOB 12:12

COMPLIMENTS

This is mighty delicious, ma'am," said Avery. "We did have us some bad luck and ended up with no breakfast this morning." I held my breath for a moment, but Avery was smarter than I gave him credit for—he said nothing at all about being chased by the Turley bull.

"Then you'd best have a piece of apple pie," answered Mrs. Turley. "Mary, cut them a piece of that pie in the window. Mind you, be careful now. It's still hot."

The pie was just as good as it smelled.

"Mrs. Turley," I said as I washed down the last swallow, "that was about the best apple pie I ever tasted."

"That's nice to hear," she said without smiling. "The way my menfolk swallow the food around here, I'm not sure whether it be good or not. They just gulp it down and leave the table."

I supposed Mrs. Turley might not be the only woman with that complaint. I decided then and there to pay a few more compliments to the cook—whoever it might be.   [64–65]

When a sincere compliment comes to mind,
don't hesitate to give it.

Well done thou good and faithful servant.
MATTHEW 25:21

OUTLOOK

Once back on the road with our stomachs full and our spirits revived, we began to pay more attention to the fall day, pointing out items of interest to one another.

We even started to reminisce about our camping trip. We first discussed all of the good things about it, like the colorful fall leaves, the fact that it hadn't rained, the clarity and freshness of the crik the closer we got to the spring. Then we started discussing the other things that had happened. We passed that old bull in the pasture, and the whole fearful experience came flooding back. But soon we were seeing the funny side of it all, and we laughed and pounded one another on the back and nearly rolled on the ground. Before we realized it we had quite convinced ourselves that our camping trip had been a tremendous success, and we could hardly wait to get home and tell everyone about it. In fact, we decided, there really wasn't one thing about it that we'd change even if we could. Well, maybe enough food for one last breakfast. [65]

> *What makes us miserable today*
> *may have us laughing tomorrow.*

> The LORD turned again the captivity
> of Zion.... Then was our mouth filled with
> laughter.
> PSALM 126:1–2

GOSSIP

I looked Avery square in the eye. I wanted to tell him how dumb he was—but he was my best friend. He flinched some at my look and scuffed his feet back and forth on the ground.

"It's got nothin' to do with likin' or not likin' Camellia," I finally said. "I don't even know her yet. Neither do you or any of those other fellas. But standin' around talkin' about her doesn't do anybody any good. We might as well be playin' or somethin'."

"I'll get the guys," said Avery, but before he turned to go he said one more thing—"You're gettin' more like your preacher uncle every day. Ever'body in town knows he won't tolerate nobody talkin' 'bout nobody."

I knew Uncle Nat didn't care none for town gossip. He had been the butt of it far too much himself as a kid growing up in a difficult situation. So maybe I had learned it from Uncle Nat. I didn't like the feel of gossipy tongues either. And I wasn't one bit ashamed of the fact.   [81]

One person who refuses to listen to gossip
can keep it from spreading.

He that goeth about as a talebearer revealeth
secrets: therefore meddle not with him that
flattereth with his lips.
PROVERBS 20:19

SELF-IMPROVEMENT

Uncle Nat brought Old Sam, the town drunk, home with him and kept him on the livin' room couch during the snow storm, but Sam left some time during the night on Friday.

Old Sam had been in our town for as long as I could remember. He had worked at odd jobs before the bottle took complete control of his life, but he didn't even try anymore. I don't know where he got money for booze. He sure never had money for food. Some of the town people gave him a meal now and then. He didn't have money for clothes either. Uncle Nat tried to keep Sam dressed so he wouldn't embarrass folk or freeze to death in the cold weather.

Old Sam was as much a part of our town as the butcher or the grocer, and everyone sort of used him as the example of complete godlessness and waste. Mamas would say to their sons, "You don't want to turn out like Old Sam, do you?" The menfolk would say that their lazy employees were "about as useless as Old Sam." And angry fellas would say to one another, "Why don'tcha go join Old Sam, where ya belong?" or "You smell as bad as Old Sam"—but nobody could do anything to change Sam from what he was.   [87–88]

Ridicule and scorn do not help people improve.

Speak evil of no man . . . shewing all
meekness unto all men.
TITUS 3:2

RESPONSIBILITY

"J osh had quite an honor today," Aunt Lou told Uncle Nat. "The teacher asked him to help his daughter, Camellia, with some geometry."

"That so?" said Uncle Nat. "Good for you, Josh. We'll co-operate in any way we can." Then he turned serious. "This might be an answer to my prayers. I called on the Foggelsons when they moved to town and invited them to join us in worship. Mr. Foggelson said they had no need nor interest in church. That it was for the deprived and unlearned—as a crutch—that educated men had things other than myths and fables to give their attention to. Maybe God can use you in some way, Josh, to bring His light to this family."

The thought kinda scared me. I was no preacher or anything. If Uncle Nat had failed to convince the man, surely there was nothing I could do. I mean, it was real scary to have someone's eternal destiny, so to speak, resting on my shoulders. [99–100]

Every day we meet people whose eternal destiny
may be affected by what we do or say.

Let every one of us please his neighbour
for his good to edification.
ROMANS 15:2

HALF-TRUTHS

"Hey, listen to this," Avery called out. "Josh went home with Camellia to *help* her with her *geometry*."

"Her pa asked me to," I wailed as I was slapped on the back and punched on the arm, my face getting redder by the minute.

"I s'pose that's why you carried her books and held her hand, too," Jack Berry taunted.

"I did not," I denied.

"An' here you were pretendin' to not even be interested in her," said Jack. "An' I s'pose you had 'tea' with her mother," he said, holding his fingers in a ridiculous pose and pretending to sip from a dainty cup.

"I did not." Then I remembered the small cups and the flimsy pastries. Well, it hadn't been with her mother. I didn't know where to start with my denying; so much of what was being said was the truth that it was hard to sort it out from the errors. A downright lie you can dismiss in a hurry, but when it gets all tangled up with a smattering of truth, it is awfully hard to untangle.   [112–113]

Mixing lies with truth is one of the oldest and most dangerous forms of deception.

The serpent . . . said unto the woman, Yea,
hath God said, Ye shall not eat of every tree
of the garden?
GENESIS 3:1

GOALS

Mr. Foggelson sat down on the desk in front of me. He had a strange look on his face—like disdain or disgust or something. "Don't ever be a teacher, Joshua," he said. "Poor pay, long hours. Day after day trying to pound a few facts into dense, uncaring little heads. You have a good mind, Joshua. I can see your face light up with understanding and appreciation. You can go far, Joshua. Be anything you want to be."

I knew he was paying me a high compliment, yet I didn't know what to say in response.

"Have you given consideration to what you'd like to do with your life, Joshua? A lawyer? A surgeon? An architect?"

I smiled confidently. "Yes, sir. A minister. Like my uncle Nat."

I guess I expected Mr. Foggelson to greet my announcement with enthusiasm, but he didn't. He didn't seem pleased at all. Then I remembered that Mr. Foggelson did not attend church. He most likely did not understand much about being a pastor.

Mr. Foggelson cleared his throat. Then he said a very unusual thing—more to himself than to me. "We'll see," he said. "We'll wait and see." [114–118]

*It is dangerous to get close
to those who are far from God.*

Blessed is the man that walketh not
in the counsel of the ungodly.
PSALM 1:1

SELF-DEFENSE

I was still getting a great deal of ribbing about tutoring Camellia. The fellas got a lot of laughs from it but they meant no harm. It wasn't that way with Jack Berry. He had been a close friend. Now he rarely even spoke to me, just about me—and everything he said was mean and cutting.

I was really sorry about this. I had never had an enemy before and I didn't like it. I knew what the Bible said about enemies—that we are to love them, to do good to them. But it sure was hard to be nice to Jack Berry. He seemed to spend his nights thinking up mean things to say about me and his days saying them. I tried to ignore the insults, but it sure got tough. Even the other fellas were beginning to say I shouldn't let Jack say those things, that I should stand up to him. I tried to shrug it off. Willie was the only one who really understood how I was feeling.

"It's tough, Josh," he said. "Doing what you know Jesus would do is really tough sometimes." Though he acknowledged that not defending myself was difficult, that was exactly what Willie expected a follower of Jesus to do. [119–120]

It is natural to defend ourselves.
It is spiritual to trust God to defend us.

Unto him that smiteth thee on the one cheek
offer also the other.
LUKE 6:29

FIGHTING

On Thursday I went to Camellia's house to study. After a few minutes of working on geometry, Camellia started talking about other things. When I finally pulled myself away, gathered up my books and my coat, and left her house, I was in a big hurry. I had chores waiting at home. I was running by the darkened schoolyard when I heard a shuffling sound. Before I could turn to look, someone grabbed me and a fist whirled through the air and hit me right in the face. I hollered out and my book went flying through the air. The fist hit me again. This time pain streaked through my right eye. It made tears stream down my face so I couldn't even see my assailant. I had never fought in my life, but suddenly I was fighting as if my life depended upon it—maybe it did. I just kept on swinging as hard as I could. And then a solid blow caught me right on the chin, and I felt my knees turn to mush.

"That oughta teach ya!" a familiar voice choked between gasps for air, and I knew it was Jack Berry who had attacked me. I tried to force my weak legs to hold me up long enough for another punch, but they refused. My head hit something solid and everything went black. [120–121]

*When anyone is forced to fight for his or her life,
the human race loses more of God's image.*

Bless them that curse you, and pray for them
which despitefully use you.
LUKE 6:28

PURITY

From the kitchen I could hear the sound of quiet voices, and I knew the rest of the family was gathered waiting for me to return to wakefulness.

"You've been sleeping for some time, Joshua," Gramps was saying. "Are you feeling any better?"

I wasn't sure. My head still hurt pretty bad but it was tolerable if I held it still.

"It's snowin'," I murmured. "How much?"

Gramps smiled. I think that simple question was a great relief to him.

"We've had about three inches already, Joshua, and it looks like we're going to get lots more."

"Good," I said. "We can have Christmas."

The earlier snow was already rutted and dirty. I had never felt that such snow was fit for Christmas, even though I realized a messy ground would not keep Christmas from coming. But for me a "real" Christmas, Christmas the way it should be, meant white freshness covering our world. I guess Gramps understood, for he grinned widely.

"We sure can, Joshua," he said. "We sure can." [127–128]

Only Jesus can bring freshness
and purity into our lives.

Wash me, and I shall be whiter than snow.
PSALM 51:7

JEALOUSY

Aunt Lou lifted my head so I could swallow the tablet with a drink of water. Then she left me alone to rest. I lay quietly and let my hand rest on Pixie's head. She slept beside me, occasionally lifting her head and licking my fingers with her warm little tongue. Soon the medicine began to take effect, but instead of sleeping deeply as I had done before, I began to do some thinking, now that the pain was dulled.

What happened anyway? Why am I here in bed? I mulled over in my mind.

Jack Berry kept flashing through my thoughts, but I had no idea why. Jack had been pretty nasty lately. He was jealous because Camellia had invited me to her house. But what did my being in bed have to do with Jack Berry? I couldn't work my way through the fog to find the answer.   [128–129]

> *If we allow jealousy any space in our lives,*
> *it swells until we explode in rage.*

> Jealousy is the rage of a man.
> PROVERBS 6:34

CHRISTMAS

I loved the snow of Christmas. It made the world look fit to welcome the King of kings—even if He did come as a tiny baby and likely didn't even notice if there was snow or not. But I couldn't imagine Christmas without snow. Once when a visiting speaker at our church said that there most likely was no snow in Bethlehem on the night Jesus was born, I wanted to argue back that the fellow must be wrong. To think of Christmas with no snow—a dirty, bare, sordid world to welcome the Christ-Child—just didn't seem right.

Yes, I waited every year for a Christmas snowfall. It was like a hallowed sacrament to me—the covering of the drab, ugly world with clean freshness right from the hand of God Himself. The unclothed trees, the dirty rutted yard, the bare, empty fields—all were suddenly transformed into silvery, soft images, always making me think that something truly miraculous was happening before my eyes. [133–134]

> *The mystery and miracle of the incarnation makes*
> *every day a Christmas celebration for the believer.*

I bring you good tidings of great joy,
which shall be to all people.
LUKE 2:10

FOUNDATIONS

After Gramps won three games of checkers I pushed the board back a bit and stood to stretch.

"Mind not on the game, Joshua?" he quizzed me.

I grinned. "You 'most always beat me. Can't always blame it on my mind bein' elsewhere."

"No not always—but this time I think we can."

"Maybe so," I admitted, and sat back down again. "Just thinkin' on some new books I been readin'—about evolution."

"Pure hogwash," he said with a snort. "Darwin got these ideas of where everything came from. He saw the similarity in the animals and birds and fish and decided that they had a common source. Well, he was right. They do have a common source. A common Creator. Only thing is, Darwin got mixed up about the beginnings. He decided that he knew more about things than anyone else and threw out what the Good Book said about God creating all things in the beginning. Try as he did to make all the pieces fit, he never did get them untangled."

We talked a long time. It was a relief to have some solid ground under my feet again. [145–146]

A solid foundation of spiritual truth
helps us understand the natural world.

The natural man receiveth not
the things of the Spirit of God.
1 CORINTHIANS 2:14

CREATION

Camellia looked at me in total disbelief. "You don't really believe that stuff about creation, do you?"

"I do—I most certainly do. God created everything. And you'd believe it too if you'd just read what it says."

"But it doesn't make sense—"

"*Evolution* doesn't make sense," I argued. "Why would things 'evolve' when their present state was not nearly as demanding?"

"Oh, Joshua—think! Don't just fall for those old superstitions that have been passed down from generation to generation. We are enlightened now! No scholars believe that Bible gibberish."

"You don't believe the Bible?" I asked in amazement.

Camellia was no longer smiling. She had a pleading look, like a woman placating a child. "Look, Joshua, we know this is hard for you, being raised in the church and—well, we are willing to take it slowly—to help you to understand. That's why Papa has let you use his library. With scientific information at your disposal, you will discover the truth for yourself."

[147–148]

Each of us must choose whether to believe man and
doubt God or to believe God and doubt man.

Who hath known the mind of the Lord,
that he may instruct him?
1 CORINTHIANS 2:16

PROOF

Papa said that you have more potential than any student he has ever had. He will help you make something worthwhile of yourself if only—"

"I think I'd better go," I said, feeling all mixed up inside. I couldn't understand all of this, but I didn't like it. Not one bit. I moved to the door, but Camellia was there before me.

"Joshua, if you go like this can't you see what it will do to my father? Hasn't he suffered enough already? He lost his position in his last school just because he tried to help some students understand true science. And now you are going to spurn his help. Don't you see, he just wants to help you."

"By takin' away the truth and makin' me believe a lie?"

"I can't believe this, Joshua," she said hotly. "You have a good mind. How can you just accept everything without thinking it through?"

"But that is what you've done. Just because you love your pa, you believe whatever he tells you without even having proof. The Bible has been proved over and over, and it never comes up short." [148–149]

It is impossible to prove anything
to someone who has chosen not to believe.

Who changed the truth of God into a lie, and
worshipped . . . the creature more than the
Creator. . . .
ROMANS 1:25

OPEN-MINDEDNESS

Mr. Foggelson wiped the chalkdust from his hands. "Camellia tells me you two had a misunderstanding last evening," he said.

"I don't think so, sir. I think we understood one another very well. Camellia believes that stuff about evolution, and I believe the Bible."

"Have you studied evolution, Joshua?" he asked, knowing I would have to say no.

"No, sir. Not really. But I've read enough—"

"Perhaps you are making your judgment too hastily. Don't you feel that you should acquaint yourself with all of the facts before making your decision?"

I looked squarely at him and tried not to flinch. "No, sir."

"And why not?" he quizzed me. "Are you afraid of the truth?"

"No, sir," I answered quickly.

"Then why did you refuse to look at what other scholars have arrived at after years and years of scientific study?"

"Because—" I swallowed again, "because, sir, it disagrees with Holy Scripture." [152–153]

Being open-minded is like driving a convertible;
it's great under certain conditions, but if you don't
know when to put the top on you'll be all wet.

And ye shall know the truth,
and the truth shall make you free.
JOHN 8:32

SCRUTINY

How do you know that your 'Bible' is accurate? How do you know that it isn't a book of fairy tales? Do you have proof, beyond all doubt?"

I didn't answer. I just sat there and shuffled my feet, swallowed, and thumbed the pages of my geography book.

"Think about it, Joshua. I would feel a failure if you, my best student, closed the covers of scientific books because you dared not challenge the teachings thrust upon you since babyhood. If the Bible is true, it should bear the scrutiny, right?"

That sounded reasonable, so I nodded.

"Well, then," said Mr. Foggelson, "I am glad we have had this talk. My library is still at your disposal. I hope you will use it and open your mind to all truth."

I gathered my books and stood up. "Good night, sir," I mumbled. I was confused about a lot of things, but of one thing I was sure. I would not go back to the Foggelsons' to use the books. There was too much I wasn't ready for yet. Maybe someday I would need to grapple with the theories they presented as fact, but not now. I wasn't ready to face them, and I had the sense to know it.   [152–154]

The words of God's created beings may fail under scrutiny, but the Word of the Creator never will.

Heaven and earth shall pass away,
but my words shall not pass away.
MATTHEW 24:35

BROKEN FRIENDSHIPS

I was just leaving the Foggelsons' yard when I ran into Jack Berry. And I mean just that. I wasn't paying very close attention to where I was going and I swung around some shrubbery and smacked right into him coming up the walk. Jack grabbed a fist full of my shirt front and pulled me toward him, his face red with anger.

"You been sneakin' around callin' on Camellia?" he hissed.

"I have not," I hissed back, jerking his hand away.

"I'll ask Camellia," he assured me, "an' if you have, you're gonna be sorry. Next time you won't get off with just a bump on your poor dumb head."

I pushed past Jack and started for home. And to think there had been a time when I counted him as one of my friends. But that was before Camellia had come to town and he had gone crazy over her. Well, he could have Camellia. I didn't care. No, that wasn't true. I still enjoyed her laughter and the toss of her curls. I still prayed for her every night.

I continued home, still riled by my encounter and trying to sort through the whole silly mess. Life sure could get complicated. How could a person put it all together?   [161–162]

> *It is better to be strangers*
> *than friends separated by sin.*

Make no friendship with an angry man.
PROVERBS 22:24

REVENGE

Spring slid from April through May and into June. After everything that had happened to me, the days seemed lazy and uneventful. At school, Mr. Foggelson's attitude toward me was either to ignore me or avoid me, and I preferred it that way. Camellia was too busy telling secrets to the other girls to pay much attention to any of us fellas. We all knew that Jack Berry was still a frequent visitor at Camellia's house.

I no longer cared. I still burned with anger every time I thought about Jack. Since my memory had come back, I had never discussed with anyone the details of the night he had ambushed me. Maybe I was afraid someone would try to talk me out of my anger, I don't know. Anyway, I nursed my anger and conjured up all sorts of evil and torturous things that I hoped would one day happen to Jack Berry. [165]

Wishing evil for our enemies makes us equal to them.

Rejoice not when thine enemy falleth,
and let not thine heart be glad when he
stumbleth.
PROVERBS 24:17

TIMING

About eleven o'clock someone knocked on our door. It was Tom Harris. I could tell he had been running pretty hard.

"Is Pastor Crawford here?" he puffed. "We need him, right away. Old Sam is dyin'. He wants to talk to the parson."

"He can't come now," I said. "Aunt Lou is havin' her baby."

"But he's gotta! Old Sam won't last long."

I was about to shove Tom out the door when I heard Uncle Nat's voice behind me. "I'm sorry, Tom. I can't leave just now. Lou needs me here, I'm sorry."

Tom left then, slowly, sadly.

It wasn't long afterward that Uncle Nat came from Aunt Lou's room with his hat and Bible. I knew he was going to see old drunken Sam, our useless town bum. Deep inside I felt that this was all wrong. I was annoyed with Old Sam. Uncle Nat had talked with him many times about making things right with his Maker, and he never would pay him any heed. Now here he was, sick and dying and deciding that it was time to clean up his life. I didn't blame Sam for not wanting to face God in his present state, but he could have picked a better time to start getting sorry for all his sins.   [170–173]

The majority of people never have
the opportunity for a death-bed conversion.

Now is the day of salvation.
2 CORINTHIANS 6:2

SERVICE

It was almost one-thirty and Uncle Nat still hadn't come home. Doc had spent most of that time with Aunt Lou. When he came back out to the kitchen, he looked old and tired.

"The baby didn't make it, Josh," was all he said.

A thousand questions hammered at my brain, but I didn't ask a one of them. I couldn't. No words would come. I wanted to cry, but tears wouldn't come either.

I ran to my bedroom, threw myself on my bed, and let the sobs shake me. After I was all cried out, the bitterness began to seep into every part of me. I was angry. Deeply angry. *God could have stopped all this.* If He was going to take Aunt Lou's baby, He could have left Uncle Nat with her to share her sorrow. But, no, Uncle Nat was out caring for some old drunk who had never listened to him. So Aunt Lou had been all alone. Why? Didn't God care? Didn't He look after those who followed Him? After all, Aunt Lou and Uncle Nat were serving Him. One thing I knew for sure, I would never be a minister. Not for anything. If a man couldn't even count on God to be with him and look after him, what was the point of spending your life serving Him?   [174–175]

> *Our motive for service must be to give, not to get,*
> *or we will always be disillusioned.*

> With good will doing service, as to the Lord,
> and not to men.
> EPHESIANS 6:7

HUMAN JUDGMENT

When I awoke the next morning, I heard voices coming from the kitchen. I could hear Grandpa, then Gramps, talking in soft tones to Uncle Nat. When I finally forced myself to enter the kitchen, I saw that Uncle Charlie was there, too.

"Mornin', Boy," said Grandpa, and he reached out an arm and pulled me to himself. He just held me close, like the holding would somehow lessen our pain.

I don't know when Uncle Nat returned. Whenever it was, it was too late by my way of thinking.

"You'll be happy to hear that Sam asked God to forgive him last night," said Uncle Nat.

I nodded. I knew that was good, but I just couldn't get too excited about it.

"Doc is carin' for him now. He's much better this mornin'."

"He didn't die?" I sputtered in bewilderment.

"No. He had himself a good scare though."

Old Sam had called Uncle Nat away from Aunt Lou and then not even had the decency to die. As soon as he was back on his feet he'd be right back to his sinful ways, I'd wager. It made me even angrier.   [176–177]

*Only God knows whether or not
a sinner's confession is sincere.*

Not everyone that saith unto me, Lord, Lord,
shall enter into the Kingdom of heaven.
MATTHEW 7:21

HYPOCRISY

One day I went to the grocery store for Aunt Lou and nearly ran into Camellia on my way out. She stopped and gave me one of her special smiles. "Would you care for some ice cream, Joshua?" she asked.

"Sure," I said. "I'll have some with you."

At the sweet shop, we settled ourselves at the counter on one of the high stools and gave our order.

"I suppose you've heard I am no longer seeing Jack," Camellia said casually. "He was just so dull. Papa never could endure him. Papa just detests a person with no wits, and Jack certainly was witless."

I couldn't have agreed more, but I didn't say so.

"Papa says he thinks Jack has chalk dust where his brains should be," Camellia laughed. "He was just so boring. He couldn't reason a thing out for himself. Why, he couldn't even follow the thinking of a person who could reason. He never will make anything of himself."

I sat there not saying anything. I hated Jack Berry. Yet it didn't seem right for Camellia, who had supposedly liked him, to say such harsh things about him. [180–181]

Polite actions that cover hatred are evidence
of hypocrisy, not Christianity.

It was not an enemy that reproached me;
then I could have borne it.
PSALM 55:12

GOD'S WILL

I haven't really talked to you about the baby, have I, Josh?" Aunt Lou asked. "We were wrong about her birthing time, you know. She was full term. She died because she had some terrible deformities. Doc says that I was already expecting her when I had the measles. Measles can cause serious abnormalities in babies if the mother gets them in the first few months.

"Every day I thank God that He took our baby home to be with Him," Aunt Lou continued, and tears filled her eyes now. "Every day."

"But I heard you that night. You said, 'Please, God, no.'"

"Yes, I did," agreed Aunt Lou. "My faith was small, Josh. I admit that to my shame. When I saw the baby and was afraid that she would live with her handicaps—her deformities—I said, 'Please, God, no'—not because I was afraid she might die, but because I was afraid she might live. I cried out to God to take her. I was wrong, Josh. I should never have done that. I should have been willing to accept from God whatever was right for us and our baby. I did pray for the strength to accept God's will—later," went on Aunt Lou. "And I was finally able to honestly say, 'Thy will be done.'" [183–185]

The first step toward knowing God's will
is accepting it.

And be not conformed to this world: but be
ye transformed by the renewing of your mind.
ROMANS 12:2

SOVEREIGNTY

Aunt Lou stood up and brushed away her tears with her apron. "I know this has been hard for you, too, Josh," she said. "You wanted that baby 'most as much as Nat and me. But we'll make it, Joshua. With God's help, we'll all make it."

I got up to go. I had wood to split and haul. I was glad, too, to be out of the kitchen. I was really confused now. We had lost our baby, but Aunt Lou said she thanked God every day for His mercy in taking her. How could I have known that God—in His will—had been answering Aunt Lou's prayer when He took Amanda Joy to heaven?

But I was still upset about Uncle Nat being away. If God wanted to care for Aunt Lou, He could have had Old Sam get sick at a different time. There was no reason Aunt Lou should have been left to face the delivery of a severely deformed child, then the loss of it, all alone. Surely God could have worked things out much better than that.   [185–186]

If we want everything to go our way,
we can't have a sovereign God.

And [Jesus] said, Abba, Father, all things are
possible unto thee; take away this cup from
me: nevertheless not what I will, but what
thou wilt.
MARK 14:36

TRUE FRIENDSHIP

Willie rode his old horse Nell over for a visit one day. We spent our time rubbing down the old horse and talking about our summer. Already we were talking camping trip again. All our bad memories of the first one had pretty much faded.

"You know," remarked Willie, "I understand Avery lots better since that trip. We spend lots of time together now. Was a time when I couldn't understand what you saw in him. Now that I know him, I really like him."

Willie went on. "His ma is feelin' lots better now, an' I think Avery feels better about things, too. He's grown a lot closer to God now that he isn't so scared. I think God worked out that trip so I could get to know Avery better and he'd have one more good friend."

Willie's words made me do some thinking. I had a feeling that Willie might be a much better friend for Avery than I had ever been. Willie was helping him to understand God better. I had left Avery to do that all on his own. [191–192]

If our friends don't know God better
for having known us, we are not a good friend.

Paul, an apostle of Jesus Christ by the
commandment of God our Saviour,
and Lord Jesus Christ, which is our hope.
1 TIMOTHY 1:1

FAITH

Willie sliced his rock against the surface of the pond. "Did ya hear that the School Board is lookin' for another teacher?" he asked. "They didn't like all the stuff Mr. Foggelson was teachin'. Like evolution an' everything. That's why he got kicked out of his last school, ya know."

"Yeah," I replied. "I heard. When are they leavin'?"

"He's still tryin' to convince the Board to let him stay," Willie answered. "Don't think there is much chance, though. Some of the members are really upset about it. They say it wouldn't have been so bad if he had taught it as theory, but he's been teachin' it as fact. That's what they don't like."

"What do you think?" I asked.

"I don't think he should teach it as fact either. It mixes up some of the younger kids an'—"

"I don't mean that," I cut in. "I mean, do you think it coulda happened that way? Like evolution?"

"Isn't what the Bible says. It's a lot harder for me to believe in evolution than in a Creator." [192–193]

When it comes to understanding the origin of the earth, we must have faith in someone— God or man.

It is better to trust in the LORD than to put confidence in man.
PSALM 118:8

GOOD DEEDS

You hear about Old Sam?" Willie asked. "He asked to be church custodian—without gettin' paid—just as a thank you to God for cleanin' up his life while there was still time. He's over there cleanin' an' polishin' every minute he gets. He's doin' a good job at the livery stable, too. They gave him a raise already. They wanted to see first if he'd really be dependable— or iffen he'd just go off drinkin' again when he got his first wages. He didn't. An' Mrs. Larkin says he's a good boarder. Keeps himself an' his room nice and tidy an' comes to meals on time. He even helps some around the place."

I stopped throwing rocks and looked at Willie.

"Well, if that don't beat all," I declared, feeling some grudging gratitude toward Old Sam. I knew it sure would help Uncle Nat out a powerful amount. He'd been doing the janitorial duties at the church along with all his other work.   [193–194]

> *In God's accounting ledger, our deeds of mercy*
> *have as much value as our cash.*

I beseech you therefore, brethren, by the
mercies of God, that ye present your bodies a
living sacrifice, holy, acceptable unto God,
which is your reasonable service.
ROMANS 12:1

FORGIVENESS

There's talk in town about Jack," Willie announced. He left an' was plannin' to make himself rich real fast to impress Camellia and her pa. Well, I guess he tried—but not in the right way—and landed himself in jail?"

The whole thing hit me as funny. I threw back my head and laughed. "It couldn't have happened to a nicer guy."

Willie gave me a stern look. "What's wrong with you, anyway? What's so funny about a fella bein' in jail."

"Oh, come on, Willie, the guy jumped me in the dark and could've killed me. He finally got what's comin' to 'im."

"But Josh, you know what Scripture says about forgivin'."

"He doesn't deserve it," I said, not ready to give in.

"It's got nothin' to do with what he deserves, Josh. Nobody's arguin' that Jack *deserves* your forgiveness. But God doesn't reason like that. Whether you forgive Jack or not isn't goin' to hurt Jack Berry. It only hurts you."

"Me?" I said in shock. "What did I do?"

"Hate! Revenge! Bitterness! All those things need forgiveness. God says He will only forgive us as we forgive others. I don't want you to be unforgiven, Josh." [195–197]

We cannot be forgiven if we refuse to forgive.

But if ye forgive not men their trespasses,
neither will your Father forgive your trespasses.
MATTHEW 6:15

COMPASSION

The truth of Willie's words pounded through my brain. I hadn't thought of all that.

"I gotta get home, Josh. I'll see ya Sunday," Willie said.

I watched him go. Inside I was all mixed up. I was still angry with Jack Berry. I still couldn't feel sorry that he had gone and got himself thrown into prison. But then I started to think about what it would be like to be in a big city all on your own and be locked up in some jail, not knowing anyone and being shut away from the green grass and the blue sky. I guess I wouldn't like it much. *But he deserved it*, I kept telling myself. And then my mind flipped to some of the things that *I* deserved. I thought about my anger, hate, evil thoughts, selfishness—as bad as what Jack was in jail for.

The whole thing was confusing. I didn't know what to think about anything anymore. I turned to the pond again and started throwing rocks, but my heart just wasn't in it. None of them "skipped." They just smashed into the blueness of the pond, then sunk to the bottom. [197–198]

Compassion for others comes when
we see ourselves as God sees us.

By mercy and truth iniquity is purged: and by
the fear of the LORD men depart from evil.
PROVERBS 16:6

DEATH

When the sun swung to the west, Gramps and I decided to head on home.

"How do you think Lou is doing way down deep inside?" Gramps asked as we started down the trail.

"Good," I responded after some hesitation. "Quite good, I think. Said she thanks God that He took the baby. Said that Amanda is better in heaven. That she would have suffered a lot if she'd lived."

"She's right, Joshua. There are many things worse than death. I know it is hard for those left behind. I still miss your great-grandmother terribly, but God helps me and gives me strength and grace for each day." Gramps stopped to wipe his eyes, and then he went on. "That's not just a pretty phrase, you know, 'strength and grace for each day.' No, those are words with a lot of meaning. A lot of truth. When one is ready to meet his Maker, prepared and forgiven, death is a welcome thing. I would not wish your great-grandmother back to endure the suffering of this world. Not to bring me comfort for even one day, one hour. I love her far too much for that." [200–201]

Death is frightening only because we know more about the physical world than the spiritual world.

Yea, though I walk through the valley of the shadow of death, I will fear no evil: for thou art with me.
PSALM 23:4

EXPRESSIONS OF LOVE

I thought Gramps had put aside his thinking on death, but he hadn't.

"When it comes time for me to go, I hope folks remember that I have finally had my hopes realized. I've felt lonesome for heaven for a long time now, Joshua. Ever since your great-grandmother left ahead of me. I can hardly wait to get there. Every day I have to ask the Lord for patience. No, Joshua, I hope that no one will ever grieve long for me."

I started to protest but Gramps kept right on talking. "Your great-grandmother's passing did bring about one good thing, Joshua. If she hadn't left me, I might never have gotten to know you. It's been good, my boy. I have loved our checkers, our chats, our choring, and most of all our fishing. You're a good boy, Joshua. I'm mighty proud of you."

There were so many things I wanted to say to Gramps. Like how I loved him, how much I enjoyed his companionship, his help, his just *being there*. Like how much more fun it was to come home to the farm knowing that he was there. But I didn't know how to put all those things into words.   [201–202]

> *To feel love gives pleasure to one;*
> *to express it gives pleasure to two.*

> That their hearts might be comforted,
> being knit together in love.
> COLOSSIANS 2:2

WASTEFULNESS

I'm getting to be an old man now. It won't be too much longer until the Lord calls me home to join your great-grandmother. But you are still young, Joshua. Your life stretches out before you. Don't waste it. A life is far too precious to waste.

"The most wasteful thing one can do is to fight against our Maker. His plan is the best possible plan to follow. Whatever it is, don't waste time and energy fighting against Him. Life is too short for that—even though right now it looks to you like you have almost forever. I'll be there waiting for you, Joshua, but I want you to come triumphant, because you have served God above everything. Do you understand me?"

I nodded. I thought I did. I knew Gramps hadn't said his words to upset me. He had no idea of the thoughts I had been burying deep inside. The hate for Jack Berry. The doubts and frustrations about the Bible and evolution. The bitterness about little Amanda Joy. I was glad Gramps couldn't see my heart. He would have been hurt. I loved Gramps and would have died before I would have intentionally hurt him. [202–203]

Harboring hate and bitterness is like spending
a whole inheritance on vinegar.

And not many days after the younger son
gathered all together, and took his journey into
a far country, and there wasted his substance
with riotous living.
LUKE 15:13

INNER CHANGE

I went to town at least twice a week, stopping in to see Aunt Lou and to help her with her garden. I split and carried the wood for her, too. Aunt Lou was getting stronger every day, and though she still grieved over her baby, the anguish was gone from her eyes. She could smile again and she could even laugh. I loved hearing her sing the old hymns softly to herself as she went about her daily tasks.

"Isn't it wonderful to watch Sam polish up the church?" she said to me one day as I sat at the kitchen table.

She probably thought of that 'cause I was polishing up a new fishhook I was dying to try.

"Whoever would have believed that God could change him so much."

She went and stood near the kitchen windows, one hand holding back the lacy curtains so she could watch Old Sam washing the church windowpanes.

"That's silly, isn't it? Of course God can change a man. He changed me when I asked for His forgiveness. It just shows up in different ways, that's all." [206]

> *We can change our behavior,*
> *but only God can change our motives.*

This people draweth nigh unto me with their
mouth, and honoureth me with their lips;
but their heart is far from me.
MATTHEW 15:8

Aunt Lou gave the bread one more brisk roll, then plunked it back in the pan and gave it a firm pat.

"When I think how Nat nearly didn't go that night, it scares me. He didn't want to leave me and Amanda. It was awfully hard for Nat. I had to *insist* that he put his calling to the ministry before his family. God was asking him to go to Sam! There was no one else to go, and an hour, two hours, might be too late, forever. Doc was with me. I knew I'd be all right."

I chewed on her words. *Aunt Lou* had insisted that Uncle Nat go to Old Sam. I hadn't known that.

"Poor Nat," she said. "He felt just terrible. Not only was he grieved with losing our baby, but he was so sorry he hadn't been there with me. But it was the strangest thing. I didn't miss Nat. I felt like I was there with him, sharing in his ministry to Sam, and I felt that he was here with me, sharing in the birth of our first baby. I think it was God. I think because God has made us one, and because it was a special time for both of us, that God sorta bonded us together in love even though we were apart." [206–207]

> *When we put God first, no one will feel*
> *as if they are in second place.*

> But seek ye first the kingdom of God, and his
> righteousness; and all these things shall be
> added unto you.
> MATTHEW 6:33

LIFE & DEATH

Aunt Lou reached out a hand to my shoulder and smiled. "I would have been really upset if Nat had gone off fishing or something—but it was his duty, not his desire, that took him away from me, and I can understand and accept that."

"His duty?" I muttered.

"Yes, he had to go. Sam needed him."

"You needed him, too. He left you all alone—"

"No, not alone. God was right there with me, wrapping me in His love, holding me tight when I needed comfort. It was Sam who needed Nat. He might have died without his sins forgiven and gone out into eternity without God."

"Seems like pretty bad timing to me."

"Seems like perfect timing to me," she whispered. "At the same moment I was losing the child I wanted and loved, God was reclaiming one of His children. Every time I think of little Amanda, I am reminded of the night when Sam came back to the Father. God received two children that night, Josh. One through death, one through rebirth." [207–208]

How we leave the world is more important than how we enter it.

Being born again, not of corruptible seed, but of incorruptible, by the word of God, which liveth and abideth for ever.
1 PETER 1:23

BELIEF

Summer slowly crept toward autumn. The School Board decided to let Mr. Foggelson have one more chance. I was relieved that Camellia wouldn't need to move away. I went to see her again on Thursday. Camellia and I tried to talk about books just like we had always done. It was hard for me. I had so many things churning around inside of me. On the one hand were all my doubts. On the other hand were the Bible truths I had learned from the time I was a child. I couldn't really swallow evolution and the supposed facts that it presented. It was like Willie said. It was just too unbelievable. No, try as I might, I could not believe that things just happened. I did believe in God. *There has to be a God*, I concluded.   [208–209]

Scientists have only the past on which to base their beliefs; with God, we have the future as well.

I am Alpha and Omega, the beginning and
the end, the first and the last.
REVELATION 22:13

MOTIVES

Life had me all mixed up. I cared a lot about Camellia, but if I told her I believed that what the Bible said was true, she'd tell me not to bother coming back. I was just sure of it.

Then an idea came to me. I'd pray. I'd pray that Camellia and her ma and pa would change their thinking. That they would start to go to church and believe the things the Bible taught. Then Camellia and I could still go on seeing each other.

Even as I got excited about the thought, I knew it was wrong. Sure, I should pray for Camellia. And for her folks, too. But not so I could go on seeing her. I should pray for her because I cared about her, and because I cared about her ma and her pa. They needed to turn to the Lord. They needed to recognize that there is a Creator. Things didn't just evolve. And because God really was God, He had the right to ask His creation to walk in His ways.

Wasn't there some way I could hang on to God, my anger, and Camellia, too? Did a person have to turn over *everything*— every part of life when he asked God to direct his ways? Wasn't there some way I could choose some areas where I could still be in control? [209–210]

When we pray with selfish motives we are asking God to do our will instead of surrendering to His.

Ye ask, and receive not, because ye ask amiss,
that ye may consume it upon your lusts.
JAMES 4:3

C an't you skip church for just one Sunday?" Camellia pouted. "You go to your old church all the time."

"No," I said firmly. "No, I can't. I'm going to church."

"Well, if your church is more important than I am, then—"

"I'm sorry," I said sadly, "but I guess it is."

I thought Camellia would strike out angrily. But she didn't.

"I'm sorry, Joshua," she said. "Let's not fight. If it is that important to you, then, by all means, go ahead. I'll tell you all about the picnic when you come over next week."

"I'm sorry, Camellia, I won't be comin' next week either. I can't agree with your pa's books. I can't agree that bein' smart is the greatest thing in the world either. I believe that church is important and that God is important. I've been tryin' to hang on to God and live for Josh Jones, too. It doesn't work so good. I've got a lot of things all mixed up. I need some thinkin' time." [208–212]

> When our lives are full of what we want,
> we have no room for what God wants to give us.

> Jesus said unto him, If thou wilt be perfect, go
> and sell that thou hast, and give to the poor,
> and thou shalt have treasure in heaven: and
> come and follow me. But when the young man
> heard that saying, he went away sorrowful: for
> he had great possessions.
> MATTHEW 19:21–22

GRIEF

Y er Gramps is gone, Boy," Grandpa said softly to me.

"No!" I shouted. "No!" I brushed away Grandpa's comforting hand and dashed from the room. When I finally cried myself all out, I realized I was at the fishing hole. The grass was dew-wet and the morning foggy and cold. A sudden shiver made me realize just how cold I was. Laying beside me was my choring jacket and flannel shirt. Someone had visited me— and I hadn't even noticed. I crawled into my clothes. My body was damp from the wet grass, and the flannel felt good on my back.

I walked to the crik and bent low to splash cold water on my puffy face. It had been fun to fish with Gramps. Boy, would I miss him! He had talked to me man to man.

But Gramps had said he was lonesome. That he wanted to go home to heaven. That it was hard for him to be patient, knowing that Great-grandma was waiting for him there and all. He had said something else, too. He said, "I don't want anyone grieving long for me." Strange he should say that—just a few short days before he went home. [214–215]

Grief is inevitable and painful,
but for the Christian it is only temporary.

The righteous hath hope in his death.
PROVERBS 14:32

BLAME

Gramps had talked about more than death on our last fishing trip. He had talked about life, too. About how to live it. That I was to be sure to let God have complete control of every part of my life. That meant I couldn't hang on to bitterness or anger. I couldn't hang on to my future either and make my own plans about what I wanted to do. It meant that I couldn't blame God for things that happened. Either God was God—or He wasn't. There was no moving Him in and out of my life with the mood I happened to be in.

As I thought of all of these things, I started sobbing my heart out. Only this time I wasn't grieving for Gramps. I was grieving for me. I sure had messed things up. I had filled myself so full of anger and bitterness and pain and doubts, and then I had turned right around and pointed my finger at God as though He was to blame for it all. I knew better. Deep down I knew better. How could a God who loved me enough to die for me turn around and be spiteful and mean? [215–216]

Blaming God for our disappointments is just another way of refusing to take responsibility for them.

And it shall come to pass, that when they shall
be hungry, they shall fret themselves, and
curse their king and their God.
ISAIAH 8:21

SURRENDER

I cried it all out to God, asking Him to forgive me and to take away all of the bad feelings I had inside. I told Him I was done making my own plans. That I was willing to be a preacher if that's what He wanted me to be. If He wanted me to be a farmer, I'd be that. Or if He wanted me to be a lawyer, or a doctor, or even a teacher, I would try to be the best one I could possibly be.

And then I prayed—sincerely—for Camellia and her ma and pa. I prayed that God would help them to understand how much He loved them and how sad He was that they couldn't believe in Him. I prayed for Mrs. Foggelson in another way— that she might have the courage to come back to her faith.

I even prayed for Jack Berry. All of a sudden, I felt so sorry for Jack. He had hated school, but his pa had insisted he be a doctor. He had liked Camellia, but that hadn't worked for him either. He had wanted to do great things and prove himself important, and now he was alone in some musty jail with no one to visit him or even care that he was there.   [216]

Surrendering to God gives us compassion
for those who have not yet done so.

Be of the same mind one toward another.
Mind not high things, but condescend to men
of low estate. Be not wise in your own
conceits.
ROMANS 12:16

LETTING GO

I got up and washed my face and then looked toward heaven. How could one feel joy and sorrow at the same time? Yet I did. I felt good inside—clean and good. And yet I hurt. I hurt bad. I was smart enough to know I would hurt for a long time to come. I just couldn't think of life without Gramps. But I wouldn't grieve. For his sake. He had asked me not to. He was now in heaven where he longed to be. I loved him so much that I'd let him go.

I turned my steps homeward. A feeling of peace stole over me. Maybe that was what Aunt Lou had tried to tell me about. God's love. God's love was there to hold me when I needed His comfort so much.

I took a deep breath. The whole thing was strange. I had nearly thrown away my faith when I had lost someone I loved— and here, at the loss of someone else I loved, it had been restored again.

"God works in mysterious ways," I repeated to myself. I had heard Uncle Nat say those words, but I'd never really understood them before. [217]

*Letting go of earthly attachments
is the only way to hold onto God.*

Father, into thy hands I commend my spirit.
LUKE 23:46

WINTER IS
NOT FOREVER

FUTURE

Willie's insistent voice demanded my attention. I swiveled around to get a look at him.

"What do you plan to do—after graduation?" he prodded.

I had been asking myself the same question over and over, and I still didn't have an answer. Graduation was only one month away, and it seemed that I was the only one in our small town school who didn't know exactly what to do with life after the big day. It wasn't that I hadn't given it a thought. I thought about it most of the time. I prayed about it, too, and my family members kept assuring me that they were praying as well. But I still didn't have an answer to Willie's question. I must have been frowning, and I guess Willie understood my dilemma. He didn't wait for my answer—not in words, anyway; he went right on talking.

"God has different timing for different people, and with a reason," he mused. "That doesn't mean that he hasn't got your future planned out. When it's time—" [13–14]

*God's will for the future is no different
than it is for this moment.*

A time to be born, and a time to die;
a time to plant, and a time to pluck up that
which is planted.
ECCLESIASTES 3:2

FREEDOM

I quit listening for a minute, and my mind jumped to other things. Willie already had his future clearly mapped out. God had called him to be a missionary; Willie would leave for a Bible school in the Eastern United States at the end of the summer. I envied Willie. "It must be a real relief to know what God wants you to do," I muttered under my breath.

"I still can't believe it," Willie said. "For as long as I can remember I've been goin' to school, day after day. And here we are about to graduate. I just can't believe it."

I twitched my fishing pole as if I were trying to stir up some fish. Actually I was thinking about Willie's words. It did seem strange. We had done a great deal of talking over the years about how glad we would be to graduate and leave the old school behind. We crowed about the day we'd be free from "prison." We'd run and holler and toss our caps in the air. But here we were on the brink of graduation and I didn't feel glad about it at all. In fact, I felt rather scared. [14]

Physical freedom sometimes brings uncertainty;
spiritual freedom always brings certainty.

If the Son therefore shall make you free,
ye shall be free indeed.
JOHN 8:36

UNCERTAINTY

Final exams were just a few weeks away, and our grades could have a great deal to do with our being accepted into college. Maybe that was why I was having such a difficult time. Most of the others already had a college picked and a vocation to pursue as well. Daily, it seemed, someone asked me, "What are your plans, Josh?" and I would mumble, red-faced, that I still hadn't decided for sure.

For sure? That made it sound like I had several considerations. The truth was, I was about as far from knowing what the future held for me as I had been on the first day I climbed the steps of the schoolhouse.

I avoided folks as much as I could. I didn't want to answer any questions when I still didn't have an answer.

As a result, I hung around home a lot. I pretended to be studying, and Aunt Lou and Uncle Nat certainly approved of that. I was trying, but my mind just didn't seem to want to stay with the books. [27]

It is better to be uncertain for a while
than to be wrong for a lifetime.

And thy life shall hang in doubt before thee;
and thou shalt fear day and night, and shalt
have none assurance of thy life.
DEUTERONOMY 28:66

FEAR

Uncle Nat didn't even knock. He opened my door gently and poked in his head. He was wearing his hat, something he didn't usually do in the house.

"Lou says it's time, Josh," he said in almost a whisper. "I'm going for Doc."

My mouth went dry and my breath seemed to catch in my chest. *It was time.* The very thought sent a shiver of fear running all through me. I had known all along that we would face this eventually, yet I still wasn't prepared.

For some reason the little unknown somebody that Aunt Lou had been carrying had seemed so safe and protected as long as her body enclosed it. But now it was time for this baby to enter the world—a world where sickness and dangers abounded. Would the little one make it? The loss of another baby would be too much for any of us to bear.   [30–33]

Fear often comes when we have the most to gain,
because that's when we also have the most to lose.

Fear took hold upon them there, and pain,
as of a woman in travail. . . . For this God is
our God for ever and ever: he will be our
guide even unto death.
PSALM 48:6, 14

PROTECTION

Doc laid the precious bundle in Aunt Lou's arms. The baby waved a small fist frantically in the air and went searching for it with a puckered-up mouth. She managed to connect the two and began sucking noisily. We all laughed. Aunt Lou held her even closer, and Uncle Nat's eyes filled with tears. She *was* beautiful.

"Sarah Jane," said Aunt Lou, "meet your cousin, Joshua Jones. He's about the finest cousin a little girl could ever have. You're a lucky little girl, Sarah Jane—No, not lucky—blessed." Aunt Lou gave me one of her special smiles. I could feel the firm arm of Uncle Nat about my shoulders, and it gave me a warm, family feeling.

I looked down again at the tiny bundle in Aunt Lou's arms. Aunt Lou had been like a mother and aunt all rolled up in one. Now I had little Sarah Jane, too. I loved that little bundle with all of my being, and no harm would ever come to her that I had the power to stop. [30–33]

A family is God's wall of protection around children.

Keep me as the apple of the eye,
hide me under the shadow of thy wings.
PSALM 17:8

IRRITABILITY

Are you coming to town for the social tomorrow night?" Willie asked.

It was a church social—one of the few activities meant just for our age group, and they were always fun. Aunt Lou and Uncle Nat saw to that. Most of the young people eagerly anticipated the monthly socials, and I enjoyed them, too. At any other time I would have answered Willie with an enthusiastic, "Sure, I'll be there," but instead I mumbled, "I'll see."

"Well, sure hope you can make it." Willie shifted his pole and the one fish he had caught into his left hand so he'd have his right one free to untie his horse from the hitching rail.

I hadn't been very good company, and suddenly I felt ashamed because of it. It wasn't Willie's fault that Camellia still wasn't a believer, and it wasn't Willie's fault that I still didn't know what God wanted me to do with my life, and it wasn't Willie's fault that graduation was quickly approaching with its unsettled questions. Willie had no more control of the ticking clock than I did. I had no right to be irritable with Willie.   [17]

When we're irritable with others it may be
because we're angry with ourselves.

He that is slow to anger is better than the
mighty; and he that ruleth his spirit
than he that taketh a city.
PROVERBS 16:32

FIRST & LAST

When graduation finally did arrive, I felt all strange. On the one hand I was excited about having completed high school. There were some awfully nice things said about me at the ceremony.

On the other hand, I felt all empty inside. Here I was, finishing up my schooling without the faintest notion of what I was to do next with my life. Willie was going off to train as a missionary; Camellia was going to New York; Janie and Charlotte were both setting out to be teachers; Avery was going to work with his pa; Polly was getting married—the list went on and on. But Joshua Jones, head of the class, didn't have any idea of what he would do with all this education.

My family all said that I shouldn't rush into deciding, should take my time choosing the field I wanted to pursue, as God directed me. I knew they were all still praying. I knew they were all behind me, but I was quite sure that none of them knew just how much the question of the future weighed on my mind. [48–49]

> *When we're used to being first,*
> *it's not easy being last.*

So the last shall be first, and the first last:
for many be called, but few chosen.
MATTHEW 20:16

DECISION

Suddenly something became very clear to me. As soon as I could, I excused myself from my graduation party and went to my room. I began to pack my few belongings into my duffle bag. It was spring. Planting time. I could see the arthritis in Uncle Charlie's hands. He was in no shape to hold the reins. Grandpa would never be able to do all the planting alone. They needed me at the farm. I could sort out my future later. I thanked God for putting it off for a while. We could work it out later, the two of us; but for right now I had a job to do.

I hurried faster as I packed, the emptiness within me filling up with anticipation. I loved the farm. I'd plant this one crop before I moved on. There wasn't time now to get any other help for Grandpa, and he needed his crop. If I didn't help him, who would? Scripture did say, after all, that we are to honor our parents. Grandpa wasn't really my parent, but he was the only father I had ever known. I figured that was what God meant when he spoke the words.

The decision felt right to me; and I had the impression that God approved of it.   [49–50]

> *Having wrestled with a difficult decision,*
> *we will have more strength for the next one.*

I will go in the strength of the LORD God:
I will make mention of thy righteousness,
even of thine only.
PSALM 71:16

DIRECTION

Y ou plan to farm again next year?" Uncle Nat asked.

I shrugged. "I guess so. I mean, I still don't know what else I'm supposed to do, and Grandpa still needs me." There was silence for a few minutes and then I spoke again. "Do you think I'm wrong? Do you think I should be tryin' harder to find out what God wants me to do with my life? It's not that I don't want to know, or don't want to obey Him."

"Are you happy here?" Uncle Nat asked.

"Yeah, I guess I am."

"You don't feel uneasy or guilty or anything?"

"No." I could answer that honestly. I was still puzzled, still questioning, but I didn't feel guilty.

"Then, Josh, I would take that as God's endorsement on what you are doing," said Uncle Nat. "For now, just go ahead and keep right on farming. If God wants to change your direction, He'll show you. I'm confident of that." [63]

God has nothing to gain by misleading those who want to follow Him.

Lead me in thy truth, and teach me:
for thou art the God of my salvation; on thee
do I wait all the day.
PSALM 25:5

THE BEST

Uncle Nat and I tucked away the empty lunch bucket and moved to the creek for a drink of cold water.

"Josh," said Uncle Nat as we turned to go for the horses, "while you are here, you be the best farmer you can be, you hear? Find out all you can about soil, about livestock, about production. Keep your fences mended and your buildings in good repair. Make your machines give you as many years of service as they can. Learn to be the best farmer you can be, because, Josh, in farming, in preaching, in any area of life, God doesn't take pleasure in second-rate work."

I nodded solemnly. I wasn't sure how much time God would give me to shape up Grandpa's tired farm before he moved me on to something else, but I knew one thing. I would give it my full time and attention until I got His next signal. [63]

Whatever our job,
God's will for us is to do our best.

And whatsoever ye do in word or deed, do all
in the name of the Lord Jesus, giving thanks to
God and the Father by him.
COLOSSIANS 3:17

AUTHORITY

My feelings for Mr. Foggelson hit an all time low. How could he do this to the girl's mother? And how could he do it to Camellia? If she was really homesick, did he think that he was all she needed at Christmas time?

I couldn't even speak for a few moments. The angry thoughts were churning around inside of me. I felt more compassion for Mrs. Foggelson at that moment than ever before. Her husband had robbed her of so much—her faith, her self-esteem, and now her only child. I wondered just what kind of account he would give before God on the Judgment Day.

"I'll keep in touch," I promised Mrs. Foggelson.

"And Josh, keep praying—please," she pleaded.

I nodded. I wasn't sure if she meant to pray for Camellia, or for herself, or that she would soon see Camellia again—or all three, but I'd pray. I'd pray lots and often. Living with a man like Mr. Foggelson, she really needed prayer. [68–69]

If we use our authority to walk on people,
we can't expect them to stand on their own two feet.

As an eagle stirreth up her nest, fluttereth
over her young, spreadeth abroad her wings,
taketh them, beareth them on her wings: So
the LORD alone did lead him, and there was
no strange god with him.
DEUTERONOMY 32:11–12

POSSESSIVENESS

I left the dining room and wandered to the room that had been mine for so many years. It sure looked different. Aunt Lou had everything so neat and tidy, with new curtains on the window—white and frilly, not the kind a boy would have enjoyed. Little throw cushions were propped up against the pillows, too.

I stood there for a few minutes looking around me and thinking back over the years. Then I pushed the door shut and knelt by the bed. "Father," I prayed, "you know how I feel about Camellia, and how sorry I am for Mrs. Foggelson. Well, I'm too angry right now to pray for Mr. Foggelson, but I do want to ask you to take care of Camellia and bring her into a relationship with Jesus . . ."

As I prayed for Camellia and her mother, my anger began to subside, and I began to realize how wrong my own attitude had been.

"Lord, Mr. Foggelson is a possessive and selfish man, and he's done some terrible things to his family. But I guess he needs you about as much as anyone I know. Help him find you, too, Lord—and help me forgive him." [70]

If we try to possess another person,
God is not in possession of us.

Neither as being lords over God's heritage,
but being ensamples to the flock.
1 PETER 5:3

GOD'S APPROVAL

I was so busy that fall I scarcely had time to miss Willie and Camellia. I needed to be in about three places at one time. There was so much to do, and only Grandpa and I to do the farming.

Grandpa had slowed down a lot, too. I hadn't realized until I was working with him just how difficult it was for him to put in a full day's work. I should have never left them alone while I went to school in town; I should have been there sharing in the responsibility. Maybe things wouldn't have gotten so far behind. But I knew they never would have agreed to my staying at home. Even now, they made comments about my "calling" and reminded me that I was not to hesitate when I felt God was prodding me on to what I "really should be doing" with my life. I asked myself frequently if I felt Him prodding, but I also found myself bargaining with Him.

"Can I wait, Lord, until I get the pasture fence mended?" I'd pray. "God, would you give me enough time to get in the crop?" And each time I asked His permission, I felt like I got His nod of approval.   [73]

If we get God's approval daily,
we don't have to fear His disapproval in the future.

Study to show thyself approved unto God, a
workman that needeth not to be ashamed.
2 TIMOTHY 2:15

BEAUTY

I had loved winter as a boy, but then I hadn't had the responsibilities of seeing that everything and everybody made it through without mishap or suffering. Winter had simply been a time of sport—sleigh rides, tobogganing, ice skating, snowfalls, and snowmen. I had loved it. Now winter was a time of struggle against the intense cold, the biting wind, the deep snow, the shortened days. The weather made it harder to chore, and the supply of winter feed and cut wood seemed to evaporate before my eyes.

Thinking of all this as I walked back to Aunt Lou's, I began to feel dejected. Then it began to snow again—huge, soft, gently falling flakes. I looked toward the sky to see the snow drift toward my face and marveled anew at the beauty of it. It might not be easy to live with winter, but it certainly was beautiful when I took the time to look closely at it. [79]

*Things that cause us grief can be beautiful if we look
at them from the right perspective—
with our faces turned upward.*

And let the beauty of the LORD our God be
upon us: and establish thou the work of our
hands upon us; yea, the work of our hands
establish thou it.
PSALM 90:17

PLANNING

Randall Thomas was a big man, about forty, with a firm handshake and a kind twinkle to his eyes.

We chatted for a few minutes, my eyes traveling over the barn and feed shed all the time I was talking or listening. It didn't look to me like there had been a feed shortage at this farm. At last we got around to talking about the winter that we hopefully had just passed through.

"Sure a tough one," the big man said. "Worst I remember seein'."

I agreed, though it was evident that I hadn't seen quite as many winters as Mr. Thomas had.

"Looks like your stock made it through just fine," I said, nodding my head toward a corral holding some healthy looking cattle.

"Sold some of 'em way last fall," he surprised me by saying. "Didn't want to wait until they only made soup bones. A farmer has to think long-range. You figure about the worst that a winter can do to you and then plan accordingly." [90–91]

*Learn from the past, work for the present,
and plan for the future.*

Go to the ant, thou sluggard;
consider her ways, and be wise.
PROVERBS 6:6

REST

Mr. Thomas's eyes glinted with interest as they met mine. "You just startin' to farm?" he asked.

I nodded, then corrected myself. "Well, I was raised on that farm, but until this year I've been doin' the chorin', not the farmin'. Grandpa and Uncle Charlie have been farmin' the land. They aren't able to do it all now so—"

He cut in. "So you are farmin', and you wanta start out right?"

I nodded again.

"Well, yer a smart boy." His hand fell to my shoulder and he gave it a squeeze.

"A man can farm his land right out iffen he plants the same crop year after year. Only stands to reason. Why, even way back in the time of the Israelites, God gave a command that the land was to get a rest ever' now an' then. Same thing now. The land needs to rest—to build up its reserves agin." [92]

Rest restores our strength;
laziness diminishes it.

Rest in the LORD, and wait patiently for him:
fret not thyself because of him who prospereth
in his way, because of the man who bringeth
wicked devices to pass.
PSALM 37:7

PLANTING SEEDS

I listened attentively. But the sun was moving on, and there was so much to learn. I felt tense, and I guess Mr. Thomas sensed it. He stopped, and his eyes followed mine to the sky. "There's too much to learn in one afternoon," he said. "You come back as often as you like and we'll pick it up from here. Tell ya what," he continued as we walked toward my horse, Chester. "You draw up a plan of yer fields. Mark what's been growing in each for the last seven, eight years, and then come see me agin. We'll see what ya should be plantin' come spring."

I stammered my thanks. I hadn't expected that kind of help.

"It's important to get good seed, too," he continued. "Some farmers try to skimp on the cost of seed. But that costs 'em more than it saves 'em. Just like it is with livestock. The Bible says, 'Ya reap what ya sow.' Now I know that wasn't talkin' 'bout the grain and the stock as much as it was what ya sow in life, but the same holds true." [92–93]

If we selfishly consume all the good fruit God produces in our lives we'll have only inferior seed to plant in the future.

Sow to yourselves in righteousness, reap in mercy; break up your fallow ground: for it is time to seek the LORD, till he come and rain righteousness upon you.
HOSEA 10:12

BAD INFLUENCES

When I got to the Foggelsons', I noticed little shoots of spring plants pointing up from the flower beds. In answer to my knock, Mrs. Foggelson came to the door. When she saw me, her face lit up and she welcomed me in with a smile.

"Josh! So good to see you," she said. I sat twisting my cap in my hands in her parlor while she rushed to the kitchen for tea. Once we were settled with our cups, Mrs. Foggelson chatted about spring, about her garden, about the hard winter, and finally about Camellia.

"Camellia quit studying interior design. She is working as a telephone operator now. I am so glad. I was so worried about her in New York. She got in with the wrong choice of friends almost immediately."

"Does she like her work?" I asked.

"Not really. But it is good clean work with good people. That's the most important thing. Camellia might be smart, and she might be independent, but she has had no experience dealing with people. Especially the kind of people who would lead her into wrong living." [98–99]

A bad influence is a good thing to avoid.

Whoso causeth the righteous to go astray in an
evil way, he shall fall himself into his own pit:
but the upright shall have good things in
possession.
PROVERBS 28:10

SEPARATION

I must have looked as shocked as I felt. I lowered my fork, scattering the last of my flaky pastry onto the white damask cloth. My eyes drifted to a picture of Camellia. Who would get the pictures, the brocade sofa, the silver tea service, the china cups? What did folks do when they separated company? How did they go about portioning out a house? A home?

"Does Camellia plan to come back home again?" I asked.

Mrs. Foggelson shook her head slowly. "Camellia does not approve of my staying here. She has always been her daddy's girl, you know. If she goes to anyone, it will be to him."

I felt so sorry for Mrs. Foggelson, but what could a young fella like me know about the way she hurt?

I worried about her as I left. Mrs. Foggelson would do fine tending her flowers. But who would be responsible for the many other things that needed tending? She hadn't made many friends in town. She would need someone. I knew Aunt Lou was busy with all her housework, the church, and baby Sarah, but Mrs. Foggelson would need some lady to talk to. I would help her all I could. And I'd get Aunt Lou. [99–101]

It is difficult to keep a home together without love,
and true love is impossible without God.

Who shall separate us from the love of Christ?
shall tribulation, or distress, or persecution,
or famine, or nakedness, or peril, or sword?
ROMANS 8:35

ANSWERED PRAYER

The crop was all in, and I had just celebrated my twenty-first birthday when I got a letter from Willie. I was pretty excited when I saw his handwriting.

I just had to write, Willie's letter said, *and share with you the most exciting news. Camellia has become a Christian. I won't tell you any more about it than that, as she wants to tell you all about it herself when we come home for Christmas. Yes, you read that right. She is going to come home to see her mother. She knows that they must get some things straightened out between them.*

I couldn't believe it! It was just too good to be true. And yet I didn't know why I found it so hard to believe. I had been praying daily for several years for that very thing to happen. I brushed away tears with the back of my hand.

Camellia was a Christian! Camellia would be coming home at Christmas! It all seemed like a miracle. Praise God! Bless Willie! [105–106]

*If answered prayer surprises us,
our praying is more wishing than believing.*

And this is the confidence that we have in
him, that, if we ask any thing according to his
will, he heareth us.
1 JOHN 5:14

GOOD FRIENDS

I suffered terribly waiting for December 21. I kept trying to imagine what it was going to be like to see Camellia again. I wondered what the *new* Camellia would be like. She was a believer now. She would undoubtedly have a new softness, a new understanding, a new gentleness to her.

I hoped she hadn't changed *too* much, though. I would have been terribly disappointed if she had put her beautiful coppery hair into some kind of tight bun or something. And I couldn't imagine her in strict, plain dresses either. Somehow they just wouldn't suit Camellia.

A glance in my mirror told me that I had changed over the years, too. I tried to think back to how I had looked at eighteen and I couldn't really remember. I knew I had filled out since then. The clothes I had worn as a teenager just hung in my closet, waiting for someone to sort through them and discard them. But somehow it felt comfortable to have them still hanging there day after day, month after month, even though I knew I would never be able to wear them again.   [113–114]

*A good friend remembers what we were
and sees what we can be.*

Iron sharpeneth iron; so a man sharpeneth
the countenance of his friend.
PROVERBS 27:17

IMPRESSIONS OF GOD

Camellia sipped her tea slowly and then set her cup aside. "I honestly don't know why you and Willie didn't give up on me long ago. I was so stubborn. So blind. I don't know why I couldn't see that you were telling me the truth all the time. That you were only interested in my good. I used to think, 'These people are dumb. They are unlearned and they have one thing in mind only, to get me to be as dumb as they are.' That's what I actually thought. It was a long time until Willie could convince me that he was really concerned about *me*. That he knew I was lost, doomed for eternity, and he cared about *me*."

Camellia twisted a coppery curl around a finger as she spoke. With all my heart I wanted to reach out and take one of those curls in my fingers but I held myself in check.

"And then this thing with Mamma and Papa happened. I couldn't believe it. I was sure it must be Mamma's fault. I hated her. I couldn't understand why she had done this to Papa. I knew she had at one time believed in God. If she could do that to my papa and still pretend to have known the truth then I wanted no part of religion." [125]

People get their impressions of God
from those who claim to follow Him.

Be ye followers of me,
even as I also am of Christ.
1 CORINTHIANS 11:1

SALVATION

Camellia sighed and flipped her hair back from her face. "Willie wouldn't give up. He kept inviting me to Bible studies and to church and we had lots of talks and arguments. Then one day I did—I'll never know why—I did agree to go to a Bible study with him. Well, that was the beginning." Her eyes shone. "And who would have ever dreamed the end? I was home alone in my room one night, reading the portion we had read in Bible study. It was John 5:24: 'I say unto you, He that heareth my word, and believeth on him that sent me, hath everlasting life, and shall not come into condemnation; but is passed from death unto life.' Suddenly I believed it. I really believed it! Somehow I understood. I was evil, I knew that, but I could, by believing and accepting, pass from death to life.

"I have always been afraid of death, Josh. I wanted life. So, alone there in my room, I turned my life over to God, thanking Him that His Son had taken my condemnation, just as the verse said."

[125–126]

The fear of death can lead to everlasting life.

He that believeth on the Son hath everlasting life: and he that believeth not the Son shall not see life; but the wrath of God abideth on him.
JOHN 3:36

Camellia looked at me with a twinkle in her eyes. "We have something to tell you," she said. "Willie made me promise not to tell until he came."

Willie stood there, a big grin on his face. Camellia took his hand and drew him into the room. Only she didn't drop Willie's hand. She stood there holding it, and I saw Willie's fingers curl around Camellia's. Then Willie dropped her hand, and his free arm stole around her waist, drawing her to him.

"Josh," he said, "because you are so special to both of us, we wanted you to be the first one to know."

I felt my throat go dry.

"Camellia and I are going to be married," beamed Willie as a radiant Camellia reached up to place a hand on his cheek.

The room seemed to whirl around and around, and I was being swept along helplessly by the tide of a dark, bottomless sea. Then, just before my head went under, I realized that I was being watched, that someone was waiting for an enthusiastic response from me regarding the announcement that had just been made. [126–128]

What causes one person great joy
may cause another great sorrow.

Rejoice with them that do rejoice,
and weep with them that weep.
ROMANS 12:15

DISCOMFORT

Not until I was alone did the truth of it all really hit me. *Camellia is getting married—to Willie.* There would never, never be a chance for her to be my girl. I had no right to even think of her in that way again.

Before me flashed her beautiful face framed by coppery curls. Her eyes flashed excitedly and her cheeks dimpled into a winsome smile. I turned away from her, shutting my eyes to blot out the image, and I buried my face in my pillow and cried like I hadn't done since I'd been a kid.

For seven days I would be forced to see Willie and Camellia—together. There would be special parties, special services, extra outings—and I would be expected to be there. They would be there, too, arm-in-arm, smiling. There was no way to avoid them. I thought of faking illness, but that wouldn't be honest. I thought of not going, but that would get me nothing but questions to be answered. I thought of saying I was too busy, but the farm work was completely caught up. In the end I did what I knew I had to do. I went. Somehow I managed to make it through. [133–134]

> *When there's no way out of a situation,*
> *plow right through it.*

> I go in unto the king, which is not according
> to the law: and if I perish, I perish.
> ESTHER 4:16

FATHERS

Willie's letter said that Camellia had been to call on her pa and had been surprised to discover that Mrs. Foggelson didn't *stay* behind—she was *left* behind. Mr. Foggelson had no intention of ever resuming the marriage. Mrs. Foggelson had written him twice asking him to forgive her for not being the kind of person she should have been and for going back on her Christian faith. She told him she would be willing to try again, but that she had to be free to be the person she had been before their marriage—a Christian. He would not agree. In fact, he told Camellia he had found someone "more compatible." It nearly crushed Camellia.

For a moment I was filled with anger toward Mr. Foggelson, but then I remembered he was a victim of lies and deceit. His false beliefs had taken him down a dark and deadly path. Only God could open his blinded eyes.

I felt terribly sorry for Camellia. How shattering it must be to discover the truth about the father she had idolized for so many years.   [146–147]

Earthly fathers fail,
but our heavenly Father never will.

Behold, what manner of love the Father hath
bestowed upon us, that we should be called
the sons of God: therefore the world knoweth
us not, because it knew him not.
1 JOHN 3:1

SCHEMES

Grandpa didn't waste time in presenting his idea to Uncle Charlie. "We got two extry rooms here. The schoolteacher gits one, the hired girl the other. That way neither of 'em are put off 'bout living in a house with three men. Then we take the board payment from the teacher an' pay the hired girl. Works good for everyone."

Uncle Charlie snorted. I knew he had some doubts.

"Where's the flaw?" asked Grandpa a little heatedly.

I leaned forward in my chair. "It's a crazy scheme. We've got no business filling our house with women. We've gotten along all of these years, and I see no reason why we still can't." I hadn't run out of steam, but Uncle Charlie interrupted.

"Let's do it," he said. "I think it's time we had a woman here in this house."

I was stunned. I couldn't believe Uncle Charlie had let Grandpa talk him into something so foolish. Then it dawned on me that Grandpa really had said very little. I had been doing most of the talking, and I might have just talked myself right into a corner. [153–157]

Good ideas sound like crazy schemes when they threaten to disrupt our routines.

There are many devices in a man's heart;
nevertheless the counsel of the LORD,
that shall stand.
PROVERBS 19:21

OMNIPOTENCE

Figure you might take a bit of teasin' showin' up with two girls, Josh?" Uncle Charlie asked me.

"Girls?" I said. "One of them is Mary and the other—well, she's just a kid."

Uncle Charlie looked surprised at my assessment.

Mary showed up first. She really did look nice. Then Matilda came down the stairs, and I couldn't believe my eyes. Her hair was gathered up away from her face and her dress was much more grown-up. She wasn't a kid after all. Uncle Charlie had been right. I might be in for some ribbing.

When we got into the buggy, each girl grabbed one of my arms and hung on for dear life. I guess they feared they might get bounced right off the seat with Chester moving along like he always does. I was hard put to handle the reins. I began to sweat. I didn't know if I had the right to pray over such things or not, but I sure was tempted.   [166–167]

God is big enough to handle small problems.

Thou hast been my defense and refuge
in the day of my trouble.
PSALM 59:16

ADJUSTMENTS

Aunt Lou called me aside. "Josh," she said, "don't pay any attention to your friends." She nodded in the direction of the boys who had been razzing me for bringing two girls. "There's not a one of them who wouldn't give his right arm to be in your position tonight."

I grinned. Aunt Lou was right.

From then on things began to change at our house. My lot wasn't so bad after all. In fact, many would have envied my situation. Mary was probably one of the best cooks in the whole neighborhood. What's more, she was gentle and caring and thought of many little ways to brighten our days.

And Matilda? Well, Matilda was Matilda. She was vivacious and witty and bright—a real chatterbox, about as different from Mary as a girl could be. Each added to our household in a special way.

I wasn't chafing anymore. There were still times when our big farm kitchen seemed a bit too small and I longed for a bit more space and a little more quiet, but generally speaking we all began to adjust to one another.   [168–169]

Learning to get along with people is part of
the preparation we need for heaven.

By pride cometh contention:
but with the well advised is wisdom.
PROVERBS 13:10

MUSIC

At first the ride was rather quiet, with only an occasional comment followed by some laughter. A shooting star caused some oohs and aahs from the girls. Mary mentioned that Matilda had a lovely voice and begged her to sing a song. Matilda began to sing, softly at first, and then Mary joined in, and the beautiful sound drifted out over the moondrenched countryside. It was a well-known hymn, and by the time they got to the second verse I could hear Grandpa humming along with them. Then he stopped humming and began to sing, and then Uncle Charlie joined in, softly, shyly.

Matilda gave me a little poke, and I sang, too—a bit hesitantly at first, and then much more bravely. Soon we were all singing, full voice. We finished the song and went on to another one and then another and another. As soon as we completed one, someone would lead out in another.

All the way home we sang. I had never had an experience like it in all my life. Somehow in the singing we had drawn closer together against the coldness and the darkness of the world around us. It all seemed so natural, so right. [181–182]

When voices join in song,
lives blend in harmony.

Praise ye the LORD. Sing unto the LORD a
new song, and his praise in the congregation
of saints.
PSALM 149:1

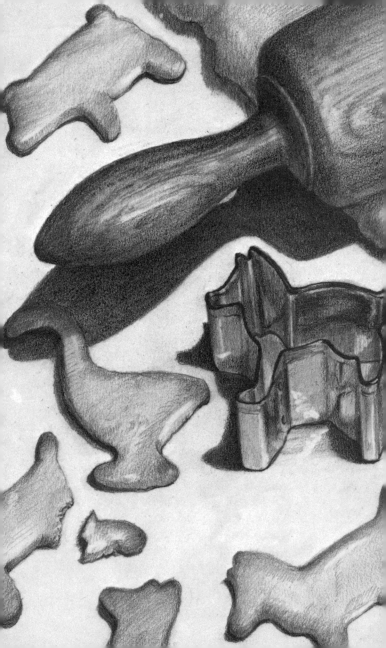

IMPATIENCE

Sarah came to visit. It had been a long time since she had spent time with us at the farm, and we had missed her.

"Oh no!" said Uncle Charlie in mock horror. "What am I gonna do with *two* bosses in the kitchen?"

Mary and Sarah both laughed.

I came home from town midafternoon to find Mary and Sarah elbow-deep in flour as they rolled and cut sugar cookies. "What would you like us to make for you, Uncle Josh?" Sarah called.

Without hesitation I answered, "A tractor." The tractor I had ordered seemed to be taking an interminable time to come.

"I thought you didn't need a tractor 'til spring," she said as she patched up the leg on a cookie dog.

"I don't."

"Then why are you so apatient?"

She tipped her head to the side and sucked some cookie dough off a finger as she waited for my answer. I waited, too. I wasn't sure how to answer her. At last I had to smile.

"I'm 'apatient,' " I said, borrowing her word, "because I *want* it so much, not because I *need* it so much."   [182–183]

Impatience can cause wise people to do foolish things.

But thou, O man of God, flee these things;
and follow after righteousness, godliness, faith,
love, patience, meekness.
1 TIMOTHY 6:11

PROSPERITY

I couldn't believe anyone could feel as bad as I felt. My whole body ached, and I broke out in sweats and then shivered until the bed shook. I was so weak that I could hardly turn my head on the pillow. Mitch Turley had to do our chores for a whole month and a half. My recuperation time did give me a chance to get back into some books. I had been so busy using my muscles that I had almost forgotten how to use my brain. I began to read Matilda's newspapers and found some articles under "Farm News and Markets."

There was so much more to farming than mere sowing and reaping. I could see the possibility of the farm turning a tidy profit in the future, and the thought filled me with energy and excitement. Folks like Willie needed support to stay on the mission field. I didn't say anything to the family yet, but I did do some talking to God. I was beginning to get a vision of the farm being used in God's work to help meet the financial needs of missionaries—especially Willie. I intended to do all I could to make the farm produce so that he would never need to worry about support.   [192–194]

*The only good reason for making lots of money
is to give it away.*

Charge them that are rich in this world, that
they . . . do good, that they be rich in good
works, ready to distribute.
1 TIMOTHY 6:17–18

SENSELESSNESS

I'm afraid I have some bad news," Uncle Nat said. "It's Willie. He's gone, Josh."

"Gone? Gone where?"

"Word came to the Corbins by telegram this morning. Willie died of Malaria a couple days ago."

"There must be some mistake!" I hardly recognized my own voice, hoarse with shock.

"There's no mistake, Josh," he assured me. "The mission board sent their deepest regrets. Willie is dead."

I heard crying, and I realized it was my own. I buried my head in my arms and the sobs shook my whole body.

"Not Willie!" my voice was saying over and over. "Dear God, please, not Willie."

It was a long time until I was able to get some measure of control. It seemed so unreal, senseless. Willie had hardly arrived out there, and now he was *gone*.   [205–206]

Only God can make sense out of senseless tragedies.

> For my thoughts are not your thoughts,
> neither are your ways my ways, saith the
> LORD. For as the heavens are higher than the
> earth, so are my ways higher than your ways.
> ISAIAH 55:8–9

COMFORT

I found the Corbin family tear-stained and desolate. Mrs. Corbin held me tightly, and I knew she was trying to hold on to a little part of Willie.

Mr. Corbin paced back and forth across the kitchen floor, his face hard and his hands twisting together. Other family members huddled in little groups here and there, whispering and crying by turn. Then SueAnn, who had been crying just like the rest of them, wiped her tears, took a deep breath, and managed a weak smile.

"I know God doesn't make mistakes," she said. "There will be some good, some reason in all this, even if we can't think of any right now."

Gradually the tears subsided and the praise started. Soon the whole atmosphere of the room changed. Someone brought out the family Bible, and they began to read, passing the precious book from hand to hand as they shared its truths.

When I left, the Corbin family was still grieving, but each member had found a source of comfort. [207–208]

What belongs to God,
we can never really lose.

Blessed be God, even the Father of our Lord
Jesus Christ, the Father of mercies, and the
God of all comfort; who comforteth us in all
our tribulation.
2 CORINTHIANS 1:3–4

COMMITMENT

I went with Mrs. Foggelson to meet Camellia's train. There was nothing we could say to each other. I just held her and let her weep, and my heart nearly broke all over again. The three of us walked home through the chill winter air and Mrs. Foggelson set about making a pot of tea.

"Your ma says you need to go back soon," I said to Camellia. "You're still set on nursing?"

"Willie said that is the biggest need out there—and who knows? If there had been a nurse there, Willie might not have died. But at least I'll have the joy of serving the people he learned to love."

It finally got through to me then. Camellia was still planning to go to Africa.

"You're going to go after *this*?" It seemed out of the question.

"Of course," she said simply, as though I shouldn't even need to ask. "They need me." [209]

> *When God calls us to meet a need,*
> *He'll meet ours.*

> I have chosen you, and ordained you, that ye
> should go and bring forth fruit, and that your
> fruit should remain.
> JOHN 15:16

A SINFUL WORLD

Does Willie's early death seem a waste to you, Josh?" Uncle Nat asked.

I said nothing.

"I don't understand about Willie's death," he continued. "It is sad and it causes us all much pain, but it wasn't wasteful. God doesn't make mistakes, Josh."

"That's what SueAnn said the day we got word of his death. But that's really hard for me to swallow. Look at Willie—if anybody was being faithful to God, he was. So why did God let him die like that, so young, with so much ahead of him?"

"Josh, none of us can know for certain *why* these things happen. We may never know. Because God gave us a free will and we chose to sin, we now live in a world marred by sin—"

"But Jesus' death sets us free from sin!" I protested.

"As individuals who trust him—yes. From the *judgment* of sin. But as long as we live on this earth, we will have to live with the effects of sin."

[216]

The task of every believer is to fight
the effects of sin in the world.

Defend the poor and fatherless: do justice to
the afflicted and needy. Deliver the poor and
needy: rid them out of the hand of the wicked.
PSALM 82:3–4

138

ACCOMPLISHMENT

"Willie's life accomplished what it was meant to accomplish," Uncle Nat said. "Willie was right where God wanted him to be at the time God wanted him to be there. He was obedient. God can only fulfill His plan for us when we obey him—about the small daily decisions and the big ones. Do you feel that you are disobeying God in farming, Josh?"

"No," I answered. "I really don't."

"Then if you are not disobeying Him, could it be that you are *obeying* Him?"

I stared at Uncle Nat. Then I began to chuckle. "It seems so simple," I said, tossing a handful of straw into the air.

"Maybe it is. Maybe we make it complicated."

A great burden had been lifted from my shoulders. *God wants me to be a farmer—the best one possible*, I thought. *Until He shows me something else.* At last I had the big issue settled. I could get on with some of the other decisions a fellow has to make.

As we headed for the house, I studied the farm I loved. A distinct feeling of spring filled the air. [217–218]

A small task, done in obedience to God,
is a big accomplishment.

A certain poor widow . . . threw in two
mites, . . . And [Jesus] . . . saith . . . this
poor widow hath cast more in, than all they
which have cast into the treasury.
MARK 12:42–43

SPRING'S GENTLE
PROMISE

FULL GROWN

I would always think of the farm as *ours*—Grandpa's, Uncle Charlie's, and mine—though in truth it really was just mine now. Yesterday Grandpa and Uncle Charlie signed all the papers to make the farm mine. *Joshua Chadwick Jones* the papers read, clear as could be. The full impact had yet to hit me. But I was excited. Really excited.

It was a big responsibility, though, 'cause now I was the one who had to make the farm "bring forth." Had to support Grandpa and Uncle Charlie and myself. I had to make the right decisions about which crops to plant and which field to plant them in, which livestock to sell and which ones to keep, and where to find the particular animal that would help build up the herd. I would need to keep up the fences, repaint the buildings, work the garden, keep the machinery in working order, watch out for weeds, put up the hay for winter feeding. . . . The list went on and on—but that didn't dim my spirits. It was a beautiful morning. I was a full-grown man with a place of my own.

[13–14]

Spiritual maturity, like physical maturity,
brings added responsibility.

Put away childish things . . .
1 CORINTHIANS 13:11

MORNING

My roots were buried deep in this countryside I had known since childhood. This was my life. My whole sense of being and knowing and living and growing were somehow wrapped up in the soil that stretched before me.

I opened the gate at the end of the lane and spoke to the milk cows. The little jersey rubbed her head against me gently as she moved to pass by. I ran my hand over her neck. She seemed satisfied then, and I smiled. *She's a great little cow,* I gloated. *Can fill the milk pail with the richest milk I've ever seen.* She was a mite spoiled, though. Her former owners had treated her as the family pet.

I hurried ahead of the cows to open the barn door for them. I knew they were right behind me, anxious to reach the milking stall where their portion of morning grain waited. They also wished to find relief from the heavy load of milk that swelled their udders and slowed their walk.

I started whistling, and a bird joined me. I turned my head to look for it and spotted it high in a poplar tree by the hen house. Its vigorous song told me that it was as happy with the early morning as I was. [14]

Being in tune with God and His creation
makes a song with beautiful harmony.

I will sing aloud of thy mercy in the morning.
PSALM 59:16

PRAISING GOD

I positioned the pail under the separator for Mary and turned to go back to the other chores. On my way to the barn to pick up the remaining pail of milk, I stopped by the tractor and ran a hand over its still-shiny fender. I could hardly wait to crawl up into the seat and begin passing back and forth over my fields, dropping the seed that would mean a bountiful harvest. I lifted my eyes toward heaven, and an unspoken prayer of thanks welled up within me.

I turned back to the chores at hand. I was whistling a tune I had learned back in my childhood, a tune I had sung frequently over the years. It swelled in my heart in a new way now: "Praise God from whom all blessings flow. . . ." [18]

Praising God for health and prosperity
keeps us from becoming proud.

Forget not all his benefits.
PSALM 103:2

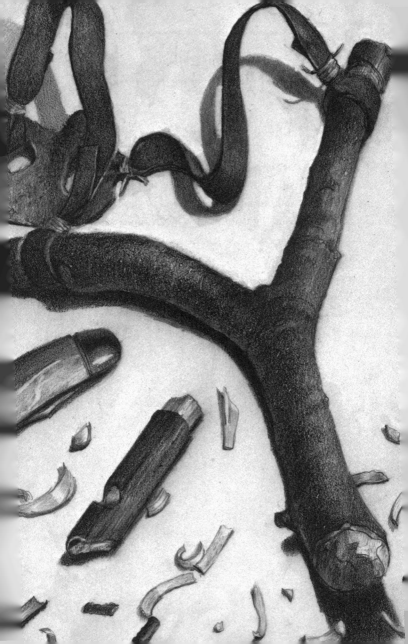

LEARNING

Mary made arrangements with Lou, and before the week was out, Sarah and and her little brother, Jon, joined us at the farm. Sarah busied herself copying Mary. She helped bake bread, churn butter, and wash clothes. She even spent time in the garden pulling weeds—along with a few carrots and turnips.

Jon tried to help, too. He dumped all the hens' water and filled their drinking dishes with hay—he said they looked hungry. He tied the farm dog to a tree using so many knots that it took Grandpa most of an afternoon to get him released— he was afraid "Fritz might get runned over by the tractor." He picked a whole pail of tiny apples that were just beginning to form nicely on the apple trees—he wanted to help Mary with an apple pie. He visited the hen house and threw a couple dozen eggs at the old sow who fed in the nearby pen—he wanted to teach her to snatch food from the air, "like Pixie."

Grandpa and Uncle Charlie tried to keep Jon entertained. They whittled him whistles and slingshots and found him a barn kitten. But in the few days he was with us we all spent most of our time undoing chores rather than doing them. Jon did not intend to be naughty, he was "just tryin' to he'p." [29–30]

> For thousands of years God has been working to undo
> the damage Abraham caused when he tried to help
> God.

Learn to do well.
ISAIAH 1:17

GENEROSITY

Mary went into the final stages of putting up summer fruits and vegetables. As I watched the stacks of canning jars fill and refill the kitchen counter top, I wondered how in the world the five of us could ever consume so much food. Part of the answer came when I saw Mary and Grandpa load a whole bunch into the buggy and send it off to Aunt Lou. Lou was too busy with her little family and being a pastor's wife to do much canning of her own, Mary reasoned. Lou was deeply appreciative. After all, a pastor's salary didn't leave much room for extras, though I'd never heard Lou complain. [37]

God gives more than we need
so we can give to those in need.

He that hath a bountiful eye shall be blessed;
for he giveth of his bread to the poor.
PROVERBS 22:9

DECISIONS

I began to find little pamphlets and newspaper advertisements scattered about the kitchen telling about motor cars. I didn't have to guess who was leaving them about, but I did wonder how Matilda was collecting them.

I read the descriptions—just like she knew I would. Some of them were fancy! Then I would look at the price. The same number of dollars could do so many things for the farm. I began to realize that Matilda's little campaign might come to nothing. It could be sheer foolishness for me to buy a car.

I went into harvest debating back and forth. One day I would think for sure I "deserved the car." The whole family deserved a car after all the years of slow team travel. *And think of how much valuable time we'd save*, I'd reason. Then the next day I would think of the farm needs, of the church needs, of my promise to support Camellia in her missionary service, of the stock I could purchase, or the things for Mary's kitchen; and I would mentally strike the motor car from my list. Back and forth, this way and that way I argued with myself. Even all of the praying I did about it didn't put my mind at rest. [37–38]

When we only want what we need,
we are on the right road to spiritual maturity.

Delight thyself also in the LORD: and he shall
give thee the desires of thine heart.
PSALM 37:4

STEWARDSHIP

The crop turned out even better than I had dared hope. I watched the bins fill to overflowing with healthy grain. God had truly blessed us. Now, how did He want me to spend what He had given? How could I be a responsible steward? I spent hours poring over the account books. There would be a surplus. But would there be enough for the motor car? And if so, was a motor car necessary? Practical? Right?

I went to my room one night and took out all the advertisements again. I laid aside the one showing the shiny gray Bentley. It was far too fancy and costly. I laid aside a few more as well. As the pile of discarded pamphlets grew, a bit of the pride and envy of Joshua Jones was also cast aside. At last I was left with a plain, simple car made by the Ford company. There was plenty of money for the Ford—with a good deal left for other things we needed. I would get the Ford. My conscience could live with that. [38–39]

*Being the best we can be doesn't require
having the best the world can make.*

If therefore ye have not been faithful in the
unrighteous mammon, who will commit to
your trust the true riches?
LUKE 16:11

VALUE

*Y*ou've always been such a dear friend, Josh, to both Willie and
me. I appreciate your friendship now more than ever. And I can never
thank you enough for helping with my support so I can go to Africa
as Willie and I had planned. I pray for you daily. May God bless
you, Josh, and grant to you the desires of your heart, whatever or
whoever that might be.

Camellia had underscored "whoever," and I could picture
her face with the teasing gleam in her eyes as I read the message.
I felt empty inside. Would anyone ever take the place of
Camellia in my heart? I read the last paragraph again, and the
idea of a motor car paled.

"Lord," I admitted in a simple prayer, "I've got things a bit
out of perspective. We need a car. I've weighed the purchase
this way and that way, and for all involved it seems like the
right move—but help me, Lord, not to get too wrapped up
in it. A car is, after all, just a way to get places. These people—
these Africans of Camellia's—they are eternal souls. Brothers.
Remind me to spend more time in prayer for them as Camellia
goes to minister the gospel to them."   [42–43]

What we value reveals how valuable we are to God.

Charge them that . . . they . . . not . . . trust
in uncertain riches, but in the living God.
1 TIMOTHY 6:17

WANTS & DESIRES

I crept back to my room, my stomach still churning and my body tight with tension. I had been repelled by every word I'd heard. *So Will is courtin'? But who? Matilda? Or Mary? And if he's courtin', then we might lose one of the girls.* The thought was not a comforting one. Matilda and Mary seemed to sort of come as a set. And furthermore, they *both* belonged to us somehow.

But no. That was ridiculous. Even I knew that. The day would come—maybe much sooner than I liked to think—that we would lose one or maybe both of them. We couldn't possibly keep the two of them forever. *Maybe we couldn't keep either one of them.* The very idea made my blood boil.

But *jealous?* Why would I be jealous? I had no claim to the girls—no personal claim. [71–72]

> *Wanting what our peers want is jealousy;*
> *wanting what God wants is righteousness.*

> Walk in the Spirit, and ye shall not fulfil
> the lust of the flesh.
> GALATIANS 5:16

COURTIN'

I didn't particularly enjoy the thought of spending my whole life as a bachelor like Uncle Charlie. I wanted a wife—love—a family. But first there came the courting. It wouldn't be hard to think of ways to court Matilda. But what about after the courting? I couldn't really picture Matilda in the kitchen, working over a hot stove, baking bread and canning the garden produce. I couldn't really see her leaning over the scrub board, hair in disarray while she scrubbed at dirty farm socks. Matilda fit into the courting picture just fine—but the marriage picture wasn't so easy to visualize.

Now Mary I could see doing all those kitchen things. I had watched her perform all the household tasks dozens of times. It seemed natural for Mary. She did it without fuss—without comment—and even seemed to enjoy it. Mary in the kitchen seemed right. But courtin'? I couldn't think of a single way to court Mary.

I lay there, struggling with questions I'd never faced before, and no matter how I tried I couldn't come up with any answers. But I knew I had to get it sorted out. My whole future depended on it. [72–73]

The right mate is worth the wait.

And Jacob loved Rachel; and said, I will serve
thee seven years for Rachel thy younger
daughter.
GENESIS 29:18

KNOWING YOURSELF

Even when I wrestled with the problem for half the night, I was no nearer an answer when I got up the next morning. I had two girls right at hand who most young men in the area considered first-rate candidates for a marriage partner, and I had been taking them for granted.

If I was going to choose one of them—and I figured I would be pretty dense not to—I needed to decide which one and get on with the courting. The trouble was deciding. They were so different—yet both special.

Matilda's energy and enthusiasm made the house seem alive. We all enjoyed her company. Even Grandpa and Uncle Charlie counted the days until she returned from her trips home. The world just seemed like a nicer place when Matilda was around.

Then I thought of Mary. Mary was quiet—not bouncy. But Mary was—well—supportive. She was dependable and sort of comfortable to be around. I'm not sure how we would have managed without Mary.

Matilda or Mary? How was one to decide? And just what kind of tension would it put on our household if I started to court the one and left behind the other? [75]

It's impossible to know the right person to marry without first knowing yourself.

Wise men lay up knowledge.
PROVERBS 10:14

154

CONSOLATION

I looked into Mary's tear-filled eyes. "How's your ma?" I asked. "Could I—"

"She's gone, Josh."

I held Mary close, letting her sob against my chest and weeping right along with her. I heard my voice on occasion but all I said was, "Oh, Mary. Mary. I'm so sorry. So sorry."

The funeral was two days later. Mitch came home, but he stayed only a couple of days and then returned to the city. Mary stayed for an entire week. It seemed forever. When she did return to us I hardly knew what to say or do. How did one share sorrow without probing? The only thing I could think of was to make things as easy for her as possible.

Whenever I saw tears forming in her eyes, I wanted to hold her again—to protect her from her pain and sorrow. [81–82]

When we wrap our arms around those who sorrow,
we do so on behalf of Jesus, who would do it if He
were here.

Wherefore comfort one another
with these words.
1 THESSALONIANS 4:18

BY ACCIDENT

Mary went home to her pa and sister Lilli. I missed her something awful at our house, but it did make things a bit easier in regard to courting. Mary said that her being home with her pa would work out good because it would help to keep tongues from wagging. I hadn't even thought on that, but if it made Mary feel more comfortable with courting, then I was quite happy to put up with it for the summer.

I was in for a great deal of good-natured teasing when family and friends learned that I was courting Mary. I didn't mind. It was nice to be known as a couple. Made us feel that we really belonged to each other in some way.

I took a hammer and mallet to the frame of the Ford and to the fender dents. It wasn't a good job, but when I was done she could at least stand on four wheels and make it slowly down the road again. I even bought some paint and touched up the scars, but she never did shine and sparkle the same. I didn't like the way she looked, but it didn't matter to me as much as I thought it would. The accident, dreadful as it was, had brought Mary an' me together.   [107]

What seems accidental may be providential.

But as for you, ye thought evil against me;
but God meant it unto good.
GENESIS 50:20

MISUNDERSTANDING

Mary was angry with me. Mary, who never got angry with anyone—who always found some explanation for the dumb things I did—who fought for me, defended me. She was angry— and I had never had Mary angry at me before. I should never have come to her house at such an unearthly hour, not in the rain that dripped muddy puddles all over her floors. I had been inconsiderate and stupid. I had been thinking only of my own loneliness.

Mary was speaking again—and there was a tremor in her voice. "I waited for you all last evening—all this evening. I knew you weren't busy. There was nothin' you could do in the rain. But you didn't come. An' finally I—"

But I had stopped listening to the actual words and was hearing the meaning loud and clear. Mary wasn't angry with me because I had come. She was angry with me because I hadn't come *sooner*. [114–115]

> *If we fail to communicate,*
> *we also fail to understand.*

Let not then your good be evil spoken of.
ROMANS 14:16

PROPOSAL

I slipped my arms around Mary and buried my face in her hair. "Mary," I whispered, "I came because I couldn't stand being without you any longer. I was so upset about the weather I didn't want to burden you with it all. But I can't bear it without you. I want you to marry me—as soon as possible. I can't stand being apart like this. Please forgive me for coming so late."

Mary turned in my arms. "Oh, Josh!" she cried. "What are you saying?"

"I guess I was asking you to marry me, but not at all like I had planned. I've just ruined the whole thing. I had these great ideas. I spent hours thinking about it. Selecting just the right words. Not just—blurting it out. I'm—I'm sorry."

Mary touched my cheek. "Sorry for missing me? For loving me?"

"No. But for spoiling what should be a treasured memory. For blundering into something that should be very special."

"Josh," said Mary softly, "I have just been told that I am loved. I have been asked if I will share your life. Josh, it doesn't get any more special than that." [115–116]

True love is more than sweet nothings.

Whoso findeth a wife findeth a good thing,
and obtaineth favour of the LORD.
PROVERBS 18:22

MARRIAGE

Mary made life totally different for me when she came home to our house as my wife. I had always enjoyed field work, but now I could hardly wait to get in from the field at night. I looked toward the house a dozen times a day to try to catch a glimpse of her. And she often slipped out with a drink of cold water or fresh buttermilk. She even came to the barn when I was milking and laughed as I squirted milk to the farm cat. She chattered about her day or her plans for the house or garden while I did my chores.

Grandpa and Uncle Charlie were glad to have her back as well. Uncle Charlie seemed to walk a little jauntier, and Grandpa took to chuckling a good deal more. Though I was quite willing to share Mary's return with them, I marveled at the fact that she was really mine—just mine—in a very unique and special way. Every day the word *marriage* took on a new meaning for me, and I thanked God over and over for Mary and that He had thought of such a wonderful plan. [129–130]

Through the eyes of marriage we see
a picture of Christ and the church.

Husbands, love your wives, even as Christ also
loved the church, and gave himself for it.
EPHESIANS 5:25

CHERISH

After our wedding I looked up the word *cherish* in the dictionary: "Cherish—to hold dear, to treat with tenderness, to nurse, nourish, nurture, foster, support, cultivate."

I read the definition again—and again. *I had promised before God to do all that?* It seemed to me that my loving Mary was beyond my control. I mean, who could help but love Mary? But "cherish"—that was different. Most of the words in the definition were words of choice, of action—not feeling.

I knelt beside our bed with the dictionary open before me, and I went over each word in the list one at a time, promising God in a new way that with His help I would fulfill my promise to Him and to Mary. I even did some thinking on just how I might keep the promises. I prayed that God would help me to be a sensitive and open husband for Mary.   [130]

> *Young lovers think love controls them;*
> *mature lovers know they can control love.*

[Love] suffereth long, and is kind.
1 CORINTHIANS 13:4

HOLIDAY SPIRIT

Winter came—according to the calendar—though the look of things didn't change much. There was no snow to speak of. The weeks trailed on, following one right after the other, and the world outside was just the same—brown and bare. Mary kept talking longingly about snow, and I must admit I was wishing for a good snowfall, too.

Christmas was nearing, though it was hard to get in the holiday spirit without a white world outside. But family members began sneaking around to hide things. Secret whisperings and plottings made life interesting and fun. The whole house began to smell like a bake shop as Mary turned out special cakes and cookies.

Mary talked about trimmings for the tree, and I hoisted the boxes down from the attic. I'd never realized before what a sorry lot they were. Mary set to work making new ones and even spent some of her egg money to replace several items. I could see that she received a good deal of pleasure out of making Christmas special for all of us. [133–134]

Jesus makes Christmas special for us,
so we make it special for others.

Glory to God in the highest, and on earth
peace, good will toward men.
LUKE 2:14

POTENTIAL

The pond in the pasture was frozen, and we took some time to slide back and forth. Sorta like being a kid again.

I thought of Willie—maybe because he had skated with me on this very pond. Boy, I missed the guy. It still didn't seem real to me that he was gone—actually in heaven. I could see his face so plainly, could hear his banter and laughter—could sense his feel of mission and commitment when he spoke of the needs of African villages for the Gospel.

I thought of Camellia, who had gone across the ocean to Willie's people. We got an occasional prayer letter from her. The Africans were poor people, and many had physical needs. Camellia was glad God had called her to this work. I still had a hard time picturing her trudging through destitute villages, visiting dirty, unkempt huts with medicines and love. But God did wonderful things with those who obeyed Him. He used people in ways we would never have dared suggest. [136]

God sees more potential in us
than we see in ourselves.

Ye have not chosen me,
but I have chosen you.
JOHN 15:16

BEING RIGHT

I drove directly to where we had left the tree—but it wasn't there. Nor were the two trees we had braced it against. I couldn't believe my eyes. I started looking around, this way, then that way, and the more I looked the more confused I got. All the time I was searching the sky was getting darker and darker. And I was getting madder and madder. It was my own dumb fault, but I was mad at Mary. She hadn't done anything to be mad about, I guess. Just been right. Anyway, I kept on looking, too mad and too proud to give up. I couldn't think of anything more humiliating than showing up at home without that Christmas tree.

But in the end I had to give up. I was so confused I didn't know which direction to point old Barney in to get him back to the barn. That made me even madder. I finally conceded defeat and let Barney find his own way home.

Mary ran to meet me as soon as I pulled into the yard. If she was disappointed about me not finding her tree, she didn't voice it.

[139–140]

Being right but handling it wrong will make a bad situation worse. Being wrong and handling it right will make a bad situation better.

Wilt thou not cease to pervert
the right ways of the Lord?
ACTS 13:10

TEMPER

I should have felt great. Half my chores had been done for me. But it didn't make me feel great. It made me even madder. *Don't they think I can even do my own work?* I fumed.

I put Barney back in the barn and fed him. No soft words or appreciative pats for him tonight. I pushed a barn cat out of the way with my foot. He was lucky. I felt like kicking him. On the way to the house it hit me. I was acting like a spoiled child, not a married man—and certainly not like a Christian husband who had promised to *love* and *cherish*. Mary had done nothing to deserve my wrath. She was trying to make Christmas special. For me, for Grandpa, for Uncle Charlie. She had wanted a special tree. Had tried hard to help me get it. It wasn't her fault I couldn't find my way around my own woods.

But she had been right, and she likely would look at me with I-told-you-so in her eyes. *If she does—*

But I stopped right there beside the woodshed and prayed, reminding myself of all of my promises and asking God again to help me keep them. It didn't change my circumstances any, but it did make me a better supper companion.   [140–141]

It is better to lose our pride than our temper.

Let every man be . . . slow to wrath.
JAMES 1:19

ONENESS

Mary had the box all ready. She had lined it with some soft material that made Pixie look as though she were all cuddled in and snug as she liked to be. The lid was next to it, and I knew Mary expected me to put that in place after I'd told my little dog goodbye one last time. I ran my hand over the silken fur and then placed the lid on the box. I pulled on my heavy mitts and looked at Mary.

"I thought you might like to be alone," she said softly. I nodded, surprised that she knew me so well so soon. I picked up the little box and went to the garden. After I completed my sorrowful task, I stayed outside for a while finding little chores I could do. When I finally was ready to face the family and go on with life, I went back to the kitchen.

Mary's eyes met mine, and we spoke to each other without words. I knew it would be a long time until I got over my hurt. Mary knew it, too. I could feel her love and understanding even when a whole room separated us. It was a marvel, this being man and wife.

[154–155]

Oneness in marriage makes us
twice as strong and half as vulnerable.

For this cause shall a man leave father and
mother, and shall cleave to his wife: and they
twain shall be one flesh.
MATTHEW 19:5

A PLEASANT SURPRISE

Mary was propped up on two pillows. Instead of being pale, now her cheeks were flushed.

"Are you really sick?" I managed.

"No," Mary answered, and her eyes were shining. "I'm just fine." She smiled, then giggled. I was about to die of worry and she sat giggling like a silly schoolgirl.

"Josh," she began, and took a deep breath to try to calm herself. "How would you like—like to be a father?"

"I'd like it," I stammered. "You know I would."

"Good," squealed Mary, "because you are going to be one!"

"You mean—now?" I yelled back, grabbing her by both shoulders. Before she could answer I jumped up, ran down the hall, and bounded down the stairs. "We're gonna have a baby!" I shouted to Grandpa and Uncle Charlie, who were both on their feet and hollering along with me. Then I ran back up the stairs again and grabbed Mary. I held her close, and we laughed and rejoiced together. [159–160]

Discomfort may be the prelude to a blessed event.

Even we ourselves groan within ourselves,
waiting for the adoption, to wit, the
redemption of our body.
ROMANS 8:23

GOODBYES

The banker was agreeable, and Pa Turley sure was, so the Turley farm now belonged to the Joneses. Pa acted like a heavy burden had been lifted from his shoulders when I handed him the check for the farm. I knew he felt that he wasn't really giving up the land—just handing it on to his family.

Mary and I drove Pa into town to catch the train for Concord, where he was going to live with his sister. When we got into town he excused himself and said he'd like to take a bit of a walk before the train pulled in. I figured he might have some old friends he wanted to say goodbye to or something—and then I saw him head off in the direction of the cemetery. He was going to say goodbye to Mrs. Turley. Guess he missed her more than any of us knew. More than he'd ever miss the farm.

The tears flowed with the goodbyes. And then the train was pulling off and we were alone on the platform. I took Mary's hand and led her from the station. More than ever, she was mine to care for now.   [163–164]

> *If we don't know the suffering of saying goodbye,
> we can never know the joy of saying hello.*

Sorrowing most of all for the words which he
spake, that they should see his face no more.
ACTS 20:38

BIRTH

According to Doc, things progressed quickly. For me it seemed to take forever. But it did eventually come to an end. Like a wondrous miracle—one minute we were in the throes of birthing agony, and the next minute we were parents. *Parents.* I could hardly believe it even though I'd been waiting for months. But there he was—*our little son*—mine and Mary's. Red and wrinkled and wailing his head off.

I kissed Mary and smoothed the tangled hair back from her face. Oh, how I loved her. How I loved that new little bundle she had just presented to me. Our very own son.

"Isn't he beautiful?" Mary crooned, her hours of pain totally forgotten. I had to admit that he was. *There's different kinds of beauty*, I thought as I looked into the little face all scrunched up with his efforts to cry.

Mary stroked him and the crying ceased. "I'll bet he's all tired out," she whispered. "It's hard work being born." [170]

Spiritual birth is sometimes a slow and painful process, but the joy of conversion makes it worthwhile.

A woman when she is in travail hath sorrow,
because her hour is come: but as soon as she is
delivered of the child, she remembereth no
more the anguish, for joy that a man is born
into the world.
JOHN 16:21

173

APPRECIATION

I rode all afternoon—from farm to farm, and the story was always the same. No one had feed. No one had money. Over and over I heard the same words.

"Boy, I'd like to, Josh. Been wantin' to get some of yer stock fer a long time. But right now ain't a good time. Crop too poor. No feed. No money. Maybe next year . . ."

But I needed cash *now*.

By the end of the day I was emotionally drained. And I'd been unsuccessful. I would have to ship the stock, and I knew the price I got for slaughter animals would not be nearly as good as that paid for breeding stock.

I hated to go home and face Mary. I was afraid she would read in my eyes the fear I felt inside.

I tried to shake off my foreboding. We'd make it. It would just be tough for a while. All we had to do was make the bank payment and ease our way through the year until the crop was up again. We could make it. It would be good for us to have to cut back a bit. Make us even more appreciative of the good harvest—the bountiful times. [176]

We need lean times to teach us to lean on God.

And I will restore to you the years that the
locust hath eaten . . . And ye shall eat in
plenty, and be satisfied, and praise the name
of the LORD your God.
JOEL 2:25–26

DEPENDENCE

At last the days began to warm into spring. I decided to start work on the land. I didn't need to wait for the snow to melt—there was none. I didn't need to wait for the fields to dry either. The stubble was as dry as tinder. I didn't use the tractor. There was no money for fuel, so I hitched up the farm horses. I'd forgotten how much slower it was with horses. As I planted I told myself that things would be better next spring.

I came in from the field each day dusty, tired, and sometimes out of sorts. I'd hoped for a rain before I did the spring planting, but when all of the land had been tilled and was still as dry as a bone, I decided to plant anyway. If I got the grain in the ground and the rains quickly followed, I'd be even further ahead.

So I planted the seed—every last kernel I had. Placed it right there in the dry ground with the faith that every farmer must have each spring—the faith that at the proper time, within the structure that God ordained for seed time and harvest, the rain would come, the seed would germinate, and a harvest would result. [179–180]

People who depend on nature for their livelihood
know how dependent they are on God.

Sing unto the LORD with thanksgiving . . .
who prepareth rain for the earth, who maketh
grass to grow upon the mountains.
PSALM 147:7–8

DROUGHT

The hot, thirsty summer was a repeat of the previous one. As I walked about the farm trying to keep the barns and fences in order, my feet kicked up little puffs of dirt and sent them sifting up to stick to my overalls or drift away on the wind that was constantly blowing.

All summer long Mary fought to save her garden. With our finances as they were, it was even more important that she have produce to can or store in the nearby root cellar. Day by day she carried water by the pail and dumped it on her plants, coaxing them, imploring them to bring her fruit.

Toward the end of the summer another calamity struck. The well, which had served us faithfully for as many years as the farm had stood, went dry. Grandpa himself had dug it, and it had never failed before. I guess we'd always assumed that our water supply was unlimited. But now, no matter how hard I pumped, there was only a small trickle, and then we had to wait a few hours until we could produce a trickle again. [183]

> *It is just as impossible to survive without water from heaven as it is to survive without water from earth.*

> And the LORD shall guide thee continually,
> and satisfy thy soul in drought.
> ISAIAH 58:11

DISCONTENT

William celebrated his first birthday, and he did seem to enjoy the occasion. We had a whole houseful over, almost like old times again.

No fuss was made, but each family brought simple food items with them. There was even a cake for the birthday boy—and some weak tea for the adults.

Sarah appointed herself William's guardian. She hardly let the rest get a chance to hold and cuddle him. But over her protests he did make the rounds. He was walking now, faltering baby steps that made him beam over his own brilliance. He seemed to know just how smart he was and spent his time toddling back and forth between eager, outstretched hands.

It was a great day for all of us, but when it was over and a thoroughly exhausted William had been tucked into bed, a sense of dejection settled over the house. It was as though we had been released from our prison for one short afternoon and then had been rounded up and locked in again. The day reminded us of how things had been, and maybe each of us secretly feared it would never be that way again. [184–185]

A taste of what we don't have
makes us discontent with what we do have.

Oh that I were as in months past,
as in the days when God preserved me.
JOB 29:2

STRESS

W ould you read tonight?" I asked Mary.

She took the Bible from me and turned to Psalms. Given a choice, Mary always turned to the Psalms. She began with a praise chapter—one that was meant to lift my spirits and bring me comfort. It should have done that for me. I had much to praise God for. But tonight the praise seemed all locked up within me. Mary hadn't read far before I was weeping.

Maybe I had just been carrying the hurts and the worries for too long, I don't know. Maybe I'd been trying to be too brave to protect the rest of my family. Anyway, it all poured out in rasping sobs that shook my whole body. Mary joined me, and we held each other and cried together.

After the tempest had passed and we were in control again, we lay for hours and talked. Just talked, until long into the night. I don't know that we solved anything, but we lifted a big burden from each other. We shared our feelings and our fears. We joined, strength with strength, to weather whatever lay before us. [186]

Trying to carry too much
may make us too weak to carry anything.

Therefore take no thought, saying, What shall
we eat? or, What shall we drink? or,
Wherewithal shall we be clothed?
MATTHEW 6:31

LOSS OF LIVELIHOOD

Whenever I went to town there was news of another foreclosure. It wasn't as hard for those who were well established. But for those who had just invested in land or stock or new machinery, it was almost impossible to stay afloat. It saddened me, and it also frightened me. The thought kept nagging at me that my turn might be next.

I didn't know what I'd ever do if I lost the farm. I loved it. I couldn't imagine myself anywhere but on that farm. Grandpa had settled it. He and Uncle Charlie had sweated and toiled and built it to what it had become. Farming was all I knew. I was not trained for anything else. I had no other home, no other possession, no other profession. If I lost the farm I would lose far more than a piece of property. I would lose my livelihood, my heritage, my family home. I wouldn't fit any other place. [195–196]

What we own is not as important as who owns us.

For your heavenly Father knoweth that ye have
need of all these things.
MATTHEW 6:32

WEAKNESS

One midsummer afternoon I went for a long walk across my dreary-looking fields. The stalks were stunted and scarce. There was nothing to harvest—again.

I crouched down in the field and dug at the ground with a stick. Down, down I dug looking for moisture that was not there. Nothing. What had happened to our world? *Seed time and harvest. Seed time and harvest* kept running through my head. God had promised it. Had He failed to deliver on His promise?

For a moment I was swept with anger. I was tempted to shake my fist at the heavens. What had I done to deserve this? What had Mary done? We had tried to be faithful. I stopped myself. I knew it had nothing to do with that. Then the many years of trusting, of leaning on my Lord, drained the anger from me. "I need you, God," I whispered. "More than ever, I need you."

I returned to the farmyard unable to shake the feeling of impending doom. I had fought for about as long as I could fight. I didn't have much strength left. [202–203]

When our strength wanes, God's remains.

My grace is sufficient for thee:
for my strength is made perfect in weakness.
2 CORINTHIANS 12:9

DOOM

After supper everyone settled in the kitchen as usual. I tried
to busy myself with figures and plans, but my mind wouldn't
concentrate. I finally laid it all aside and climbed the stairs to
the room where my two sons slept.

What a picture they made. William clutched a teddy bear.
His dark lashes fell across unblemished cheeks, and thick brown
hair lay damp across his forehead.

Baby Daniel slept in almost the same pose as his older
brother—arms atop his blankets. Now and then he pursed his
little lips and took a few sucks as though dreaming of nursing.

I stood there looking at them and my insides went cold and
empty. *They're countin' on me. They're countin' on their pa, and
I'm goin' to let them down. Both of them—and Mary. And Grandpa
and Uncle Charlie . . .*

I'd never experienced such pain. Deep, dark, knifing pain
that brought no tears of relief.

I pulled the curtain back from the window so I could look
out over the land I had loved and worked for so many years.
There was no escaping it. We were facing the end.   [203]

*When the end is near,
so is God.*

Thou art near, O LORD.
PSALM 119:151

181

INGRATITUDE

Mary straightened her shoulders and lifted her chin. "We've come too far to give up now," she said. "There *has* to be a way."

I shrugged helplessly.

"We still have stock to sell. The teacher will be boarding again this year, and I don't need all of his money for groceries. You can take out more cord wood. We'll make it," she said. "God has seen us through this far—He won't let us down now."

For a moment I found myself wondering just what God had done on our behalf. The rains still had not come. We hadn't had a crop in three years. But Mary soon reminded me.

"Folks all about have been losing their farms, but we still have ours. We been meetin' those payments year by year— somehow. We are all still here, all healthy. We've always had food on the table an' shoes on our feet. He's seen us through all of this, an' He'll keep right on providin'."

I felt a wave of shame rush through me. God had been doing far more for my family than I'd been thanking Him for. [205]

When we don't see God working,
we're looking in the wrong place.

Because that, when they knew God,
they glorified him not as God,
neither were thankful.
ROMANS 1:21

182

LETTERS

The work camp was filled with men like myself. Desperate men—trying hard to make it through another winter in the only way open to them. Decent men—forwarding every penny they could spare back home to wives and family.

We talked about home in the evenings, after each chilling, grueling day. We lay on our hard bunks and told one another stories about our wives, our children. It was the only pleasure we had. Except for when we allowed ourselves to use one more carefully rationed page—one more envelope—one more stamp—so we could write a letter home. We lingered over those letters, pouring our love and longing into each sentence.

No one ever bothered a man who was writing. A hush fell over the bunkhouse. Writing home was a sacred rite. It was as close to the family as we could get.

Mail day was even more special. We hoarded every speck of privacy as we pored over our letter. And then we did a strange thing—we went over and over every tiny item of news it held with everyone in the bunkhouse.   [211–212]

*God expressed His love for us in a personal letter that
we are to share with the rest of the world.*

And these things write we unto you,
that your joy may be full.
1 JOHN 1:4

SACRIFICE

We had four days off for Christmas. Most of us walked fifteen miles to town after putting in a full day's shift so we could catch the train in the morning.

We had a simple Christmas with Lou's family. In spite of bare cupboard shelves, Lou and Mary managed to put together a tasty meal. The children didn't seem to miss the turkey and trimmings. They had fun just being together. That night Mary stayed up late trying to darn my socks again. She patched my overalls and sewed buttons back on my coat, but there didn't seem to be much she could do about my worn-out mittens.

"Josh," she said, "there's just no way to fix them."

I nodded. "They're fine," I assured her.

But the following morning when I joined the family at the breakfast table there was a new pair of mittens. Mary must have stayed up most of the night to knit them. They were the same color as her chore sweater, which I noticed was no longer hanging on the peg by the door where she always kept it. I tried to swallow the large lump in my throat.   [212–213]

We give ourselves because He gave Himself.

And walk in love, as Christ also hath loved us,
and hath given himself for us an offering and a
sacrifice to God.
EPHESIANS 5:2

VULNERABILITY

Reading my Bible and praying got me through that long winter. Several other men in the bunkhouse turned to worn Bibles, too. We talked about the things we were learning. It helped us put things into proper perspective.

One night I told them about Willie. About how much he had loved God and how much I had loved him and how we had named our first son after him.

"It's funny, though," I explained, "he always went by 'Willie' even though his name was William. We named our boy in honor of him, and I think of Willie most every time I look at my son—and yet, I've never been able to call him Willie. Never. Don't know why. Guess it still just hurts too much."

I'd never been able to share that with anyone before. I guess I figured no one would understand. But there was a strange friendship between those of us who shared the simple, crude bunkhouse. Maybe because we were all so vulnerable. Maybe we had nothing to hide. We all knew just where the other one was coming from. None of us had reason or cause to boast. We were laid bare, so to speak, before one another. And we needed one another. [213]

Honesty and vulnerability lead to camaraderie.

Wherefore laying aside . . . all guile,
and hypocrisies.
1 PETER 2:1

SECURITY

I was caught in a box. If I went home to Mary I would surely lose the farm. Yet I wondered how much longer I could hold on here. If only God would provide some way for me to make those payments—to hold the land. If only the rains would come so the land could produce again.

I started praying. "God," I admitted, "I'm at the end of myself. There's nothin' that Josh Jones can do to provide for a future for Mary, for my sons. I can hardly provide for the present. I don't know which way to turn, Lord. I just don't know how we can go on like this. I need them. They need me. But to lose the farm. What would we do then? Where would we go? We have nothin', Lord. Nothin'."

I picked up my Bible and opened it to a passage I had underlined. I read it again and found that God had already dealt with my problem. [218–219]

Nothing happens to us that God hasn't handled before.

Although the fig tree shall not blossom, neither
shall fruit be in the vine; the labour of the
olive shall fail, and the fields shall yield no
meat; the flock shall be cut off from the fold,
and there shall be no herd in the stalls. Yet I
will rejoice in the LORD, I will joy in the God
of my salvation. The LORD God is my strength.
HABAKKUK 3:17

GIVING UP

I read the passage again and again. It was all coming clear to me. The welfare of my family didn't depend on my strength. If so, they would be utterly destitute. I had been totally inadequate. But even more astounding, it didn't depend on my fields either, or the herds that I had so carefully built. It was God all the time—just like Mary had tried to tell me. It was God who had cared for my family—had met their needs. We didn't need anyone or anything else.

"'I will rejoice in the Lord—the Lord God is my strength,'" I kept repeating. Oh, what a freedom! I could finally let go. I could shift my heavy load onto another's shoulders. Somehow—somehow God would work it out. Somehow he would see us through. Maybe we *wouldn't* keep the farm—but if not—well, He'd help us to manage without it.

Soft snoring reached me from the other bunks, and I knew the men around me were getting much-needed rest. I continued to pray and praise inwardly until late into the night. When I rose the next morning, it was with new strength.   [217–219]

Giving up what we think is ours
allows God to give us what is His.

Whosoever shall lose his life for my sake . . .
the same shall save it.
MARK 8:35

ANOTHER CHANCE

With a trembling hand I picked up the receiver. Something must be terribly wrong. Grandpa wouldn't squander money on a telephone call unless it was extremely important. Then there was another voice. It was Mary.

"Josh, it's raining. It's been raining for three days." She started to cry.

Grandpa took the phone again and spoke the words I will never forget. "Come home, Boy," he said. "Come home. We already got some crop in. Mary an' me."

"Where'd you get the seed?"

"Bought it. Mary's been savin' pennies out of what you sent each month. And she sold her silver tea service."

I was too stunned to speak. I knew how much that tea set meant to Mary. It had belonged to her mother, grandmother, and great grandmother.

Grandpa put Mary back on the phone.

"Mary, I'm comin' home. I'm leavin' right now. I love you."

I hung up the phone and ran all the way to the bunkhouse. We hadn't lost the farm. The rains had come. God was giving us another chance for seedtime—and harvest! [220–222]

> When God gives us another chance,
> there's no risk involved.

> And God appeared unto Jacob again . . .
> and blessed him.
> GENESIS 35:9

INDEX